FUNN STUFF

by KARL ROHNKE

KENDALL/HUNT PUBLISHING COMPANY
4050 Westmark Drive   Dubuque, Iowa 52002

All photos by the author except where noted.

Cover and illustrations by Johneen Kissler.

Contents

It is required by law* to change the rules of any game found in this book at least once.

***Rohnke's Law of Immutable Funn**—"Change it or rearrange it, because all things being equal . . . who needs that?"

SYMBOLS

The following symbols, appropriately found near the title of each activity, should be used as a guideline for the way the activity is *usually* done.

ACTIVITY LEVEL

 No sweat

 Some sweat

 Top sweat

ACTIVITY AREA

 Indoor

 Outdoor

 Indoor/Outdoor

PROPS

 Props needed

 Some props needed

 No props needed

FUNN STUFF INTRODUCTION — TAKE TWO

As much as I like to generate the image of a professional child, let's get serious about this fun(n) stuff. Sure, I play games, fool around with initiative problems, create and build ropes course elements, etc., because I enjoy the fun, variety and people, but the raison d'etre behind FUNN STUFF is not entirely the fun involved.

The short, pithy write-ups herein provide a sampling of generic teaching tools that you can adapt to your own pedagogic style. The contents of this Vol. #2 anthology, tho' tinged with humor and massive tongue-in-cheek, were collected and written with occasional serious intent. I want you to like this *stuff* enough, via the printed word, that you will try it out with your students. I gain great satisfaction from knowing that this material is being passed along, particularly when it's used in a conscientiously adventurous way.

I have observed enough sadly conducted physical education and recreation classes to know that the material offered in FUNN STUFF 1 & 2 offers succor (. . . as in, "this game sucks!") to the students who have been hammered with too many weeks of floor hockey, kick ball, etc., and to the teachers who have lost interest because the students have lost interest.

This good *stuff* does not represent a panacea for teaching ills, which sad scenarios I'm not going to attempt to identify or define. However, the emphasis in FUNN STUFF on developing cooperation, communication and trust in a fun matrix represents a well established experiential approach that promotes a sense of discovery and self worth that is unfortunately missing in many learning situations.

Folks, I'm not just taking up space here, this approach is the real *stuff*. It's inexpensive, doesn't require specialized training (except the ropes course activities), life-type learning takes place, and both the participants and facilitator feel good about what's happening.

Here's an original Rohnke book bonus—offered as an incentive to get you to try an activity or two—*I will be pleased to chat with you about anything in any book I've authored; give me a call.* Notice I didn't indicate that you had to buy the book. Even if you are just perusing this introduction in someone's living-bath-bed room, take advantage of the offer. If nothing else we can share weather conditions. I travel around quite a bit, but there's a good chance that you can locate me through the Project Adventure office in Brattleboro, Vermont : (802) 254-5054; ext. 21. (If Lynn answers, ask her how she got a New York City accent in Vermont?) . . . talk to you soon.

Author's Comment

THE BOTTOMLESS BAGGIE is out of print—has been for about two years. Looking through an old copy not too long ago, I was both pleased and dismayed. Pleased that some of the articles were still topical and of current interest, dismayed that those articles were buried in a dead book.

I've decided to rejuvenate a few of the articles and reprint them in upcoming issues of **FUNN STUFF**. I'll rewrite, correct, or modernize whatever needs to be done and offer them again for those readers who never had a chance to see them in the first place. The safety article on *Demon Rings* (p. 31) in this issue is an excellent example, representing information that practitioners in the field of adventure education should know about.

Any article lifted from **THE BOTTOMLESS BAGGIE** will be followed by the parenthetically bound letters **(BB)**. I'm telling you this so that you don't think I'm trying to pull a plagiarize-yourself scam.

DISCLAIMER

Here we go again, me telling you to be responsible via a formalized sequence of bulleted paragraphs. Humor me, read it.

- Adventure curricula or activities should not be undertaken without the supervision of leaders who have successfully completed qualified professional instruction in the use of the skills necessary to implement adventure curricula or activities.

- Instruction and suggestions in this book for the construction and implementation of ropes course elements are subject to varying interpretations and the construction process is an inexact science.

- Before any attempt is made to use any ropes course elements whose construction has incorporated any of the materials contained in this book, a qualified professional should determine that safe techniques have been employed in their construction thereafter. I'm impressed you're still reading. Inspections by a qualified professional no less frequently than annually should be made to protect users against accident or injury that can result from the deterioration of materials caused by the use, abuse of the elements.

- The reader assumes all risk and liability for any loss or damage which may result from the use of the materials contained in this book. Liability for any claim, whether based upon errors or omissions in this book or defects in any ropes course, the construction of which has incorporated any of the materials contained in this book shall be limited in amount to the purchase price of this book. Thank you.

ADVENTURE GAMES

THE BUTTON FACTORY

I watched Ken Demas, PA trainer from Mamaroneck Middle School in New York, go through this bit of disjointed, histrionic madness at a workshop in Vermont. Way to go Ken, you're still as nuts as you need to be.

As the leader, ask the participants to repeat after you.

Hi! My name is BILL.

I have a life and a job in a button factory.

One day my boss came up to me and said —

"Hey Bill, you busy?"

"Heck no!"

"Then push this button with your . . ."

. . . fingers. As the leader, stand there repeatedly pushing buttons with both index fingers as if the buttons were on the wall in front of you. Keep doing this. (See photo)

Start again from the beginning with, "Hi, my name is Bill . . ." At the end, rather than saying, "Can you push this button with your fingers", substitute . . .

. . . elbows. Bring your elbows repeatedly together as if you were a chicken trying to fly. Keep doing this also. Start again from the beginning with . . . "Hi, my name is . . ." etc., and keep substituting body parts for pushing the buttons without giving up the initial button pushers; i.e., those parts of your anatomy already involved.

. . . knees. You should know what to do and say by this time.

. . . your posterior. Don't get too carried away with this one!

. . . tongue. Great finale for encouraging use of a foreign language.

And whatever part of the anatomy you think you can get away with. Don't take this poking, thrusting, jerking, twitching too far or your enthusiastic followers will begin to fade.

After . . . **tongue**, and having gone through the spiel again, when the boss asks, "Are you busy?" Bill responds, "Heck yeah!" and quits—amidst laughter and relief.

Considerations

- Do not present *The Button Factory* as one of your initial get-to-know-you activities.

- Practice *Button Factory* alone in front of a mirror. Get into it. This frenetic activity does not go over well with a timid, apologetic approach.

BOTTOM LINE (BB)

This highly active team game was initiated somewhat serendipidously during an adventure training session near Sydney, Australia. The initial "Bottom Line" was represented by a parallel pair of no-power lines that drooped usefully and uselessly across the designated activity area.

Objective

To hit a well inflated 20" diameter beach ball over a horizontally suspended (approximately 15 foot high) section of 1/4" diameter bungee cord, ten times without allowing the ball to hit the ground. If you are up for the extra preparation time it's actually more fun and challenging to string two lengths of bungee so that they are suspended parallel to the ground and one another, with about 30" in-between.

One point is awarded for hitting the ball over the top cord and two points are gained for smacking the ball through the "window".

Rules

- *Everyone* is on the same team. Is that great, or what? This is a very significant rule, don't change it.

- Each player situates themselves wherever they or the team thinks they can best serve the objective (as above); situate by choice.

- The ball can be hit as many times as desired before a scoring shot is attempted, but cannot be hit twice in a row by the same person.

- If the ball hits the ground all accumulated scoring hits are lost.

- Catching or directing the ball is not allowed, however the ball can be struck, smacked, headed, or kicked with any part of the body, even accidentally.

- Comparing final scores with other on-site ad hoc teams is generally frowned upon, however, attempting to reach a nebulous "world record" set by another equally nebulous team is encouraged by the ruling body.

- In keeping with the *Challenge By Choice* credo, whatever result a team is genuinely pleased with shall be accepted by the facilitator, and all spectators in attendance, as a proper and fairly set "world's record" for **THAT** team, on **THAT** site, at **THAT** time. Significant records of this type are traditionally not recorded and seldom referred to beyond a fortnight.

IF's to Consider

- If the wind is blowing in excess of a zephyr (approximately three miles an hour), either move inside or change the game.

- If the group numbers over 20 players, increase the action by including two beach balls. Counting ball strikes begins over at 1 after either ball hits the turf.

- If a *Dangle Do* high ropes course element is available, the horizontal rungs can be used as scoring markers. When a ball is hit between the first two rungs, one point is scored. When a ball is hit between the second and third rungs, two points are scored, et cetera. (See photo p. 3)

SPINAME

I was attracted to this activity because I like to activate multiple finger-spin tops, seeing how many I can keep going before one of them stops. The highly visual action is benignly frantic, there's some skill involved, and the next turn is only a spin away.

This spinning game is a macro variation of the tops action above using dinner plates as the rotating objects and ostensibly learning names as the excuse for playing.

Use 3–5 plates*, depending upon the group's skill level—experiment. This game can only be played after the group has spent some previous time actually learning each others names; this is essentially a name reminder game.

Spin a plate on the floor (wooden gym floors promote spinning, carpeted floors do not). This spin represents a full wrist and arm twisting motion. A decent plate spin is pure macro motion, don't try to finesse it. As you spin the plate simultaneously call out someone's name. That named person must move forward smartly, grab an available plate, spin it, and name another person. This continues until one of the plates spins to a stop. Whoever's turn is in progress when the plate stops must perform a forfeit before the plates are spun again.

Or, you can play with a single plate, recognizing that a named player must say someone else's name before they are allowed to grab the still spinning plate and re-spin it. If the plate stops before the named player thinks of another name, that person must perform the forfeit.

An appropriate forfeit might be to point out someone's name you don't know and ask the group to shout out that person's name. Another forfeit is to take all your clothes off and run around the building shouting your own name. Take your pick.

* Use only plates made from synthetic material that precludes breaking; i.e., shattering. I have submitted this genre of plates to my own "in-house" destructive testing program and can pragmatically report that the plates are indeed resistant to breaking, but are *not* shatter proof. Caveat: If you plan to duplicate my testing sequence (not a great idea) wear gloves, bala-clava, goggles, a heavy coat, and double weight pants—hold the Tevas.

SWITCHEROO

This fast moving game allows a just-met group to learn *beau coup* things about one another without having to sweat through initial face-to-face conversations.

All you need to do is ask the group to "line up in a circle", place one volunteer-like person in the center and ask that central player to frame a question beginning with the three words, "Switcheroo if you . . .", and finish the sentence with a revealing question. As in the game, *Have you ever . . . ?*, if you answer YES to a question you must move to another position within the circle. If you answer NO, cool it and stay where you are. A player can obviously answer *yes* or *no* to whatever question they want, and therein lies the attractiveness (empowerment), of the game.

Positioning within the circle might be problematic if the moving players have no way to tell where an open position is located. Solve the situation by asking each player, before the action begins, to place something identifiable at their feet. If you have a number of gym spots (as used in the initiative problem *Key Punch*), plop them at the player's feet and play away.

Switcheroo if you . . .

- were born before . . . (choose a date).

- are a vegetarian.

- are wearing socks that you have had on for more than one day.

- like asparagus.

- wear colored underwear.

- ever failed a high school course.

- won a medal.

- like to cook.

- like to eat.

- etc., etc.

This is a simple game to set up and play, but don't short change its effectiveness just because you aren't actively facilitating. Take a break, they have probably heard enough from you today anyway. Students slip into this game easily and will play enthusiastically through many questions.

Be aware that you may have to control the questions if they become too intimate, incisive, or embarrassing. To minimize censorship simply "arrange" for yourself to end up in the center, then ask some questions that are fun and of less prurient interest.

GOTCHA

Again, via the Australia/Collard connection; no props, no sweat, and simple, simple, simple.

Standing (sitting, squatting, prone) in a circle, ask each person to offer their left hand palm up, then point the index finger of their right hand down into the left palm of the person standing to their right. On **GO!**, each person tries to grab a finger with their left hand and to keep their right finger from being grabbed.

There are only about 55 essential words in this description. Sometimes I like to play with words, but other times succinct is swell.

Gotcha is a great "filler", but it won't fill up a 50 minute teaching block. I tried this gimmicky game with eighteen first graders and they LOVED it, for about five minutes.

I'M ONE TOO! (THREE, FOUR . . .)

I learned this simple game from Tim Herold during an Adventure Programming workshop at Pingree Park, Colorado.

The Set Up

Ask about 6–8 people to stand in a semi-circle, like a crescent, and number off. Ask two additional people to sit in two available chairs.

The Action

Player number one points to another player and says that player's number. That player must then point to another player and say that player's number. If a mistake is made by pointing to the wrong player or saying the wrong number the offending player must take the place of one of the seated players. A seated player then enters the game at the end of the line as number eight, and the remainder of the players move up a place to fill the empty slot of the player who made a mistake. Each player who moves must then take on the next number in line. Example: If I'm number four in line and number two makes a mistake, number two sits down and I move up a slot to become number three.

After you interpret what I'm trying to say, you might think that you have misread the rules because it seems too simplistic (or too complicated, depending upon your interpretation of Rohnke rhetoric). It *is* simple tho', and that's what makes the frequent mistakes even more funny and hard to fathom.

Too easy? Pick up the pace. There should be someone making a mistake at least every 15 seconds. Failure can be fun. I'm not just processing a platitude, it's true.

NEWSROOM

Prepare for some chaos. Making preparation for chaotic involvement itself is paradoxical, and further, preparation and chaos are antithetical. What? Try this.

Everyone in the group gets a pencil (no pens, this is a newspaper situation) and paper. In a timed five minute span everyone must learn as much about everyone else as they possibly can for the evening special report.

Information must be volunteered as freely and effectively as possible, and power listening is a must. Who records what is up to the group and must be decided upon during the five minute reporting/recording span. Who talks, who writes, who's listening, who records, who designates, etc.

After the five minutes, ask for a volunteer (or someone that the group has already chosen) to report on what has been researched and recorded. Is factual information important? Does the depth of the reporting have any significance? Is this worth debriefing? Does Big Ben have ticks? Consider, it takes a big zipper to make an elephant fly.

SPINNER

Keep the initiative game, *Pick & Choose* (**Silver Bullets**, pg. 77) in mind as you read about this variation.

Props You Will Need

- An 8'+ cylindrical cardboard section that's used for wrapping rugs around (that's not great gram-mar, but I like the way it sounds). Nothing else comes to mind that would work as well for the price, but I'm sure there must be something to substitute. Think about it.

- Three foam balls of various diameters, from small to big.

- 25' of #4 nylon cord or whatever cord you have.

- Many fleece or foam balls, at least two per player.

- Two 10' sections of slash rope or floor tape to act as throwing boundaries.

Objective

Now that you have at least mentally collected the necessary material, try this.

Picture the foam balls hung from the horizontally supported cylinder using the #4 cord. Each ball is hung at the same height. Players, standing behind the throw lines, try to hit the suspended balls with the fleece balls so that the foam balls flip up and around the cardboard cylinder over and over until the foam ball is wound all the way around the cylinder. One minute of throwing time is allowed to try and wind up all three suspended balls.

Details, Rules and Considerations

- Support the cardboard cylinder about 6' off the floor by either securing the cylinder to two volleyball standards or two trees.

- The knot used to connect the #4 cord to the cylinder must be tied tightly enough so that the cord does not spin on the cylinder. If your knot quotient is low (constrictor or strangle knots are the hitches of choice), secure the rope in place with a squeeze of hot glue.

- Now that you have the glue hot, use some to connect the other end of the cord to the foam balls. Make a small slice in the ball first, insert the cord, then squeeze in a dollop of glue, (a dollop is a tad more than a soupçon).

- Move the throwing lines either closer or farther away, depending upon the age or prowess of the participants. Throw a few fleece balls yourself to determine this distance. It's OK, you're allowed to have some fun too.

- Any thrown fleece balls remaining between the two throwing lines must remain there until the next attempt, unless they can be retrieved without stepping into the off-limits area.

- Participants may arrange themselves behind either throwing line. Part of the decision making process includes player location as to performance potential during the one minute "do-it" span.

- You can develop a scoring system for this activity, but I like the initiative problem approach of either achieving the objective or not. Reviewing topics can include:

decision making, failure/success, individual roles to benefit the group, leader/follower—and the necessity for having both.

- If the group's need is to have some frenetic, blatantly competitive fun, allow two equal groups (whatever that means) to blast away at the hanging balls from opposite sides. The first group to get all the balls wound around the cylinder WINS, and gets to unwind the balls.

**BIG TIME CAVEAT:
DO NOT USE TENNIS BALLS
IN PLACE OF FLEECE BALLS.**

FROGS & BUTTERFLIES

The spark for this game came from Ted Woodward, who was working at a children's home in Yonkers, NY when he sent this idea to me in 1989. (If you are waiting for an idea you contributed to appear, be patient, I check my files at least biyearly.) I changed Ted's game format a bit drastically, but that's because I edit this unlikely anthology of *Funn Stuff* and have to do something other than just type up ideas. Also, remember, change is the name of the game.

Frogs and Butterflies is best played on a polished wooden gym floor, in fact, don't bother playing it on anything but . . . At the beginning of the game,

half the players brandish a floor hockey stick and the other half manipulate a lacrosse stick.

- The hockey folks try to swat/sweep a well made (good stitching) bean bag so that it will glide towards and hit one of the lacrosse players in the foot (anything above the shin is a no-hit). When this occurs, the hit player heads for the sidelines, grabs a few lung-fulls of air (incidental evidence indicates that the oxygen content of ambient off-court air is invariably richer than on-court) and expresses their change of affiliation by re-entering the game with a floor hockey stick.

- The lacrosse players try to retaliate by hitting a hockey player with a *sliding* bean bag shot, also below the shin—no direct in-the-air hits allowed. Brandishing their netted stick, they can also try to capture a *moving* bean bag; i.e., the kinetic bag has to end up in the stick's net. If this capture occurs (called "butterflying the bag") the hockey person who's bean bag shot was captured, immediately switches sides and play-stick. If a hockey player is legally hit with a sliding bean bag, as mentioned above, they also head for the sideline to change affiliation and playing implement.

- Use bean bags to equal half the number of people playing the game.

- Distribute 2–3 rubber gym spots (lily-pads) on the floor as desig-nated safe areas. A player, standing on a lily pad, cannot be hit with a bean bag. No one may park on a lily-pad for more than 15± seconds. Only one player per lily-pad.

- Only incidental body contact is allowed/tolerated; i.e., hip checks are definitely out. The is a game of skill and humor. Competitive? Yes! Win by intimidation? No!

- Remaining on one side (un-hit) for the time span of this game is the sine qua non of *Frog & Butterfly* achievement.

- When everyone has had enough, the players can count-up to see which side has the most players, and draw whatever conclusions seem least appropriate, or they can head for the sidelines for a drink of water, sweaty bonding comments, and partaking of the higher oxygen content.

METAMORPHOSE

If you know how to play Rock/Paper/Scissors, this game is a cinch. If you don't know how, where have you been? Ask anyone who has been a child and the majority will supply you with the rules amidst a smidgen of nostalgia.

When I was a kid, decisions weren't made by committee or by fiat, unless you were a lot bigger than everyone else; your turn at whatever was desirable at that moment was determined by a rapid round of Rock/Paper/Scissors, or if time was of the essence a quick odds & evens finger match was the decider. But that was a long time ago when fingers were used for something other than manipulating Game Boys and Sega control buttons.

Here's a variation of that classic digital deciding mechanism gleaned from Laurie Frank at the 1st Annual Metaphorical Workshop held at Georgia College. If you want to know something about the 2nd Annual Metaphorical Workshop (or 3rd or 4th, depending upon when you're reading this) give Dr. Leon H. Gillis a call at (912) 454-0865, and ask for Lee.

Here's the game. Everyone starts off as an ersatz egg, positioning you to role play an egg. Get down on your haunches, round off your shoulders, and tuck your head down while making appropriate egg-like sounds. Also, kind of move around like an egg would if it could move; i.e., roll, until you encounter another egg. A quick round of Rock/Paper/Scissors (R/P/S) produces a winner, (no best two-out-of-three, just a one shot deal). The winner becomes a chicken and the egg remains an egg, rolling around looking for another egg to R/P/S with.

The chicken triumphantly stands up and flaps its elbows, I mean wings, thus announcing that she is ready (all chickens are she's, like it or not) to R/P/S with another chicken. After this contest (chicken vs. chicken) the champion chicken atavistically expands up the evolutionary scale to become a Velociraptor and in a game-like manner the other chicken answers the age old question about which came first by once again functioning as an egg.

Get the action? If you win a contest you advance. If you don't win, you retreat one step backward; unless you're an egg and there's nothing lower than that—except, of course, whale excrement on the bottom of the ocean, but that's stretching the point and the analogy.

Remember to actively role play each character level as to how you would interpret an egg, chicken, velociraptor responding within the game scenario. If you can't do that, then just don't play the game. No . . . seriously, the role playing *makes* the game, otherwise it's just another series of win/lose contests.

To spice up the game and make it last longer, provide a couple additional advancement stages for players to aspire toward. How about after velociraptoring, enter the Mensa-like world of Neanderthals. (Make up your own role play for this ancestral hominid.) Finally, the most adept and/or lucky players attain the expanded role of Siddartha, Power Rangers or some such pseudo-immortal status that even Carlos Castenada couldn't . . .

After having achieved immortal standing a participant no longer has to play the game of life; i.e., R/P/S. It is their role to appear omniscient, truly sage and somewhat nouveau riche as they wander about enjoying the antics of lower forms waging their petty, status achieving battles.

Continue play until everyone has achieved the role they so truly deserve, or until lunch.

INITIATIVE PROBLEMS

LE CAV

If you don't have a room, root cellar, basement, bomb shelter, or cave (cav) that is free of light and can hold at least 15 people, skip this write up unless you're up for a vicarious bit of pure dark groping. I thought that might spark your interest.

The most difficult part of this initiative problem (other than finding an appropriately sized black area), is to scope out a set of Tinker Toys and/or a Mr. Potato Head. Unless your Mom lovingly packed away your old sticks

and hubs don't count on finding a set of Tinker Toys made of wood, everything's plastic now, and expensive. Your basic plastic Tinker Toy set costs about $10.00, but that's not big enough, you need the $20 collection to fabricate the necessary initiative puzzle for *Le Cav*.

The Mr. Potato Head, as long as I can remember, has been made of plastic. If your group numbers around 10–12, the Mr. or Mrs. Potato Head will function as well if not as abstractly as the Tinker Toy set. Mr./Mrs. Potato Heads are not hard to find because of the recent film role Mr. Potato Head played in the animated movie, The Toy Story.

The idea is for you to build a Tinker Toy tower that's simple enough and challenging enough to tax the planning and communication skills of a high performance group; at least you *hope* they are high performing—medium performance is OK too. If they don't perform well at all, hey . . . you gotta make a living, right? But don't show your tower to the group. Take a photo of the tower (not right now, this is something you do last week) and only show them the photo. Take a decent picture of the tower; the problem is hard enough without an out-of-focus photo.

At the same time that you give them the photo, also give them the disarticulated Tinker Toy sections, (*only* the pieces that make up the Tower). Participants are given 4 minutes to study the photo, talk, and handle the pieces, but during this time they are not allowed to link any of the sections together.

At the end of four minutes exactly (be strict—grab the Tinker Toy sections

problems. You must allow verbal sharing of ideas, sentiments, emotions . . . as the result of having experienced something as a group, otherwise all your good facilitating and front loading (that's a buzz word for briefing) is just recreational.

Try substituting the playful pieces of Mr./Mrs. Potato Head as surrogates for the Tinker Toy sections above; it's less expensive.

This excellent idea came from Pat Rastall, the Associate Director of Colorado State University's Pingree Park. Pat won a silver completion buckle in the Leadville 100, which has nothing to do with this initiative problem, but it just blows me away that anyone can run 100 miles non-stop at over 10,000 feet altitude. Think about it!

The use of Mr. Potato Head in the above context was suggested by Joel Cryer of Austin, TX.

if they won't give them up. Tell 'em it's *your* toy!) escort the group to *Le Cav* and tell them that they have ten minutes to reconstruct the Tower in the dark. Indicate that you are starting a kitchen timer (the kind that ticks loudly) and that at the end of ten minutes a bell within the timer will ring. If the Tower has not been completed correctly (*exactly* like the photograph), when the bell rings everyone in the group will have to pay a forfeit of listening to Madonna records for 6 straight hours in the dark.

If you fail to allow for a group reviewing process (in the light) after the bell either rings or doesn't ring, you may not pass GO, or do any further initiative

QUICK LINE UP (ßß)

Use this run-around, willy-nilly activity to break some ice and provide a low-risk, low-skill, high-action sense of team affiliation.

First, you have to get the group to split themselves into four approximately equal groups. Quad grouping is easily accomplished by having everyone line up and then counting off 1-2-3-4, 1-2-3-4, etc. If that sounds like fun, you need help. Try this.

Ask each person to mentally pick a number from one to four that they would like to be, but not to say or indicate in any way what that number is. To discover how many other players share your state of numerical zen, walk up to someone and shake their hand the number of times representing the 1–4 number that you mentally chose.

If your number is 2 and someone tries to shake your hand 3 times, excuse yourself politely and continue searching. When you find a hand moving up and down congruently with yours and if that hand stops at the

appropriate number (jives with your karma), keep that soul buddy with you and, operating as a harmonic diad, try to find another free spirit vibrating on your joint frequency.

Continue linking until everyone has established their affiliation with a numerical group. If you're lucky, the groups will be approximately equal in number. (Three's are characteristically the smallest group.) If not, ask a few noncommited people to change groups to even things up. I didn't say that this grouping ploy worked perfectly, in fact it rarely does. Be flexible, people seldom care what group they end up in as long as they're having fun.

Now here's something for *you* to do besides appearing pedagogically facilitory. Stand in the middle of the gym or field (a bit off center is OK), and hold out both your arms so that your hands are pointing east and west. If you don't know east from west, any which way is fine. Ask the four groups to orient themselves around you so that one group is facing you, another is facing your dorsal side and the remaining two are ventrally positioned; like the N.E.S.W. points of the compass— wherever that happens to be.

Whichever position is chosen in relation to the way you are standing must be remembered by the group because after you move, and *only* on the word GO, the groups must re-establish themselves *exactly* to their original N.E.S.W. orientation to you. The first group to do this and concurrently shout, "Quick Line Up" is the WINNER.

Make your first couple moves simple, north, east, south, west twisting kind of thing. Then run to another part of the room or field before you shout GO! How about ending up on the side of a hill? Try standing next to a swimming pool.

Continue to play until you have achieved some ice-breaking, or you notice that the level of en*joy*ment needs more joy. Falling in the pool is hilarious, but that saturated group will probably be somewhat reluctant to continue dashing about at your whim.

If you have a few hula hoops around, try this. (You better try this because this variation is the only reason I re-penned the paragraphs above.) Give a hula hoop to each group. After you re-position yourself, and as the groups hustle to re-establish their proper orientation, "Quick Line Up" cannot be shouted until each member of the group has literally passed through a hoop. Techniques will vary. If you have enough hoops and the groups are fairly large, give each group two or three hoops. Request that each person shout out their individual hoop penetration number as they work their way from start to finish; keeps 'em honest, and helps you pick a WINNER! Gotta have winners, right? Wrong!

HALF PIPE

Take a 1/2" × 6–8' length of PVC pipe, and cut it lengthwise, in half. Slice (use a proper power saw) a half-piece section for each participant. Hack saws, no matter how much skill you apply, do not fall into the "proper saw" category.

Place a large colorful marble into/ onto the half pipe then, in conjunction with other team members, who also control a section of 1/2 pipe, attempt to move the marble from one geographical point to another (figure out an arbitrary route) without letting the marble roll off the pipe. Each player cannot move more than one pivot step from where

they begin, but can proceed with dispatch to the end of the line once their marbleistic transport has taken place.

It's not necessary, from a functional standpoint, to cut the PVC pipe sections in half. The reason for halving the pipes is to make the marble transport more visible and tenuous. If you don't have a saw, the steady hands, or the inclination, use a whole pipe, I won't tell.

It will quickly become obvious that to move the marble effectively the various half pipes (6–8) need to be juxtaposed end to end. Don't announce this operating tidbit, let the students discover what's necessary. I just didn't want you futzing around with the props and cursing

Karl for not being explicit enough.

Hands off the marble, no corporal contact with the spheroid allowed, except at the start and finish.

Consequence for dropping or touching a marble? S'up to you or simply require a restart after a certain number of drops.

Half Pipe has become a very popular initiative problem in the last year or so, and is an example of how an old problem can be refurbished, re-scenarioed, redone and presented as a "new" program tool. Welcome back.

As an historical aside, this problem was suggested to me over 15 years ago by Larry Brown from Knoxville. His initial plan was to use sections of whole PVC pipe and roll marbles down the tubes. When I saw Larry at a recent conference his latest suggestion was to use different sized marbles to represent different kinds of metaphorical problems at home or in the work place: creative thinking.

A metaphorical variation I thought about was to put a person, standing as a hub, with pipes of different lengths and different angles radiating away from him/her, say six pipes in all at waist height. Then six volunteers deposit six marbles on the pipes and let them roll toward the center person. The center person has a paper cup in each hand and it is their responsibility to try and catch all six marbles, not letting any hit the ground. Sound difficult? What's the metaphor? Think about the adventure game *Phones & Faxes—Silver Bullets;* pg. 63.

How about pouring water down six tubes and require that the center person collect a certain amount of water to be considered successful? That center person should be wearing khaki pants, and the ambient air and water temperature should be compassionately warm.

HUT, 2, 3, 4 . . .

If you just read through these paragraphs and are trying to participate mentally—won't work. This is a participatory, experiential, experimental, hands-on activity. (That's not front loading folks, it's overloading, but it gets the point across.)

Take two sections of cheap rope (you can use expensive rope if you want) and fabricate two concentric circles as depicted in the schematic surrounding these words.

Arrange your group so they are standing, evenly spaced, on the outside of the large circle. Ask them to perform either a right or left facing movement, so they are all facing in the same direction.

The object of this "team builder" is for the group to walk a minimum 90° arc of the circle outside the circle, then without stopping all must step inside the circle (into the "path") so that everyone enters the circular path *simultaneously*. Without stopping or missing a step, the group continues walking in the same direction another 90° arc inside the circumfrence then steps off the path and out of the circle, again *simultaneously*. It is not necessary for the participants to walk in lock-step around the circle, but when the step out is made, it must be in exact congruence with everyone else.

The 90° walking arc mentioned above is offered as a minimum; the group can walk the circumfrence as far as they think it's necessary before stepping into or out of the circle.

The initiative aspect of this activity is to coordinate the movement of the group so that all team members do what needs to be done toward accomplishing the goal. If anyone steps out of sequence; i.e., if stepping in or out of the circle is not exactly simultaneous, the group must begin again. This is not as easy as it reads, and therein lies the attractiveness of the problem from a facilitating standpoint.

Variations Include

- Finalizing the problem by stepping into the inner circle.

- Two groups walking in opposite directions.

- Groups change direction when the *in* or *out* move is made.

- Use more rope to increase the concentricity. (This probably isn't a great idea, but I wanted to use the word *concentricity*. I'm not even sure concentricity is a real word—sounds real.)

You may get some individual resistance because of the perceived military flavor of this exercise, but give it a try and I think you will discover it's only as militaristic as *they* make it.

THE LEANING TOWER OF FEETZA

Put away your game bag, props and play paraphernalia, here's a "back pocket" initiative problem that requires only people and a willingness to try something bizarre. But then, all of this stuff is bizarre; just wanted to remind you of that.

Ask a seated or standing group to look at their feet in a combined sort of way, just to get them thinking about *feet* and how many of those footsies are available for this initiative problem. Say, "I'll bet if you stacked all those feet you could make a foot **ped**estal ten feet high". I know that's a bit redundant, but in an amusing way—amuses me anyway.

Here's the rules, before I become tangential:

- Completion represents a stack of feet, ten feet high (120" if that makes more sense.)

- A participant cannot stack his/her own two feet together.

- The stack must be maintained for 5 seconds after completion.

- Team members are allowed to touch each other's feet and legs for "tower of feetza" support.

Considerations

- Provide decent spotting for those individuals who have committed their feetza to the top of the pile.

- This presentation and attempt works best in a room that has a ten foot high ceiling. Seeing the

actual connection between the floor and the ceiling is definitive and satisfying. If this **ped**estrian pinnacle is attempted outside, simply use a measuring device (**ped**ometer?) to set the challenge.

Another "perfect" location for this initiative is directly under a basketball hoop, which is ten feet high I'm told. You would be amazed at how much I don't know about basketball. Here's a sad fact: I used to be able to jump and touch a basketball rim. I can still do it mentally but the quick twitch muscles remaining in this ole white man's legs just don't get the signal.

How about using hands instead of feet? If the group is having trouble completing the feetza tower, suggest using hands; it's easier. Use extended hands (pinky to thumb) to make the vertical connecting tower. Ask a starting person to lie on the floor (dorsal down) and to put their thumb on their nose with hand extended. This blatantly rude pose provides a perfect start for your *handy* tower.

The name of this initiative was creatively suggested by Dave Klim.

RUDY'S PLOY

I'll bet Rudy Pucel would be the first to say that this demonstration was not his idea, but I heard it from Rudy, and he presented it well.

Ask each member of a group to take a piece of scrap paper and, with a pencil or pen, to exactly reproduce the following two verbally presented figures. The instructions are only offered once and no questions are allowed. Participants can copy each other's paper if they like; sometimes it's easier to be wrong together.

- Draw a horizontal rectangle with an arrow extending through the rectangle from the upper left hand corner down through the lower right hand corner.

- Draw a vertical rectangle with a two part squiggly line extending through the middle of the rectangle.

Nothing fancy, just like this:

Ask the participants to compare their drawings and comment on why their arrow drawings are mostly similar and the squiggly line drawings are predictably different.

Follow up this exercise with the activity, *"Four Sheets to the Wind"* (also known as *"You Tear Me Up"*) on page 238 of the book **QuickSilver**. Both exercises have to do with following directions and how people perceive things differently, even those things that are identically presented.

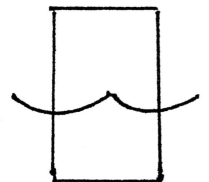
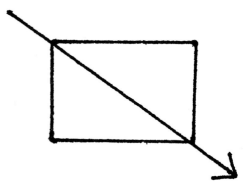

TRUST

WILD, WILD WOMEN

You better know your group really well before you present this corporal clash of the sexes. I have observed groups experiencing great fun with the physical action associated with *Wild, Wild Women*. I have also seen and heard things that would encourage you to turn this page now. Challenge by Choice, mate.

Choose a wrestling mat or a well turfed field for the potential cum kinetic action.

Ask the men in the group (yes, this is a "skins and shirts" activity) to arrange themselves in the center of the mat so that they are all making solid contact with one another; like, hold on guys. Surround this mound of males with a rope, so that the rope delineates a circular area about 10–12 feet in diameter. This measurement will obviously vary as to the size of the male bonding, (. . . just a little joke; couldn't help it.)

Alert the females that "to win" they must remove all the males from the circle. Tell the guys that they cannot fight back, they can resist, but not struggle; i.e., no wrestling.

Go!

Thanks to Charlie Harrington (former Pittsburgh Steeler rookie, currently weighing in at a solid 250+ lbs.) for this dandy game and to Richard Maizell (Howdy, Rich!) and Betty Fromley for convincing me that the game has merit—I hope.

CLIMB ALL OVER ME . . .

During the years I worked for Outward Bound (1967–1971), a favorite—between courses—evening activity was *table climbing*. Craig Dobkin reminded me of the activity a few years back and even provided me with a humorous cartoon depicting an out-of-control table climbing situation. I wrote about table climbing and how to build one (cartoon included), in the now out-of-print book, **The Bottomless Baggie;** pgs. 39–41, in case you happen to have one lying around. The object was simply to lie on top of a STURDY table, moving from the stable table top, to underneath, then back on top without receiving aid or touching the ground; simple and fun. If you are going to try a table traverse, remember to spot the climber's head and provide some type of padding under the table.

But that's not what I wanted to tell you. If anything in the paragraph above

either mean laterally around or vertically around, but whichever way is chosen, no aid can be offered to the climber. Needless to say, it would be considered gauche and wimpy to touch the ground during the traverse.

I'd suggest initially trying the lateral traverse in order to gain some confidence and sense of ease with grabbing and applying pressure to sensitive anatomical holds, because the over-the-head-and-through-the-legs traverse (see photo) can be socially delicate, to say the least. Be prepared for copious laughter, particularly from the spectators.

If the single traverse is well received, try the team traverse as depicted in the sequenced photographs on the next page. Climber Faith Evans is obviously being impelled into the classic 5.9 head/crotch traverse, and flashing it quite well in the author's opinion. Spotting is appropriate at all times, particularly when the climber is head-down or specifically requests some protection.

This activity lends itself to the age-old crag rat's conundrum, "Is it better to climb upon or to be climbed upon?" The age-old answer is up to you.

resonates with the "I've got to try it" portion of your autonomic response mechanism, try the following portable anatomic climbing ploy first.

Ask a friend who is larger than you to stand steadfast (wide base) on a thick rug or soft turf. Climb (with permission) onto the person's back, and proceed from that dorsal positioning to "climb" around their anatomy. *Around* can

WALLETS

P/2

Have you ever come across the word vademecum? A wallet is a vademecum, so is a pocket knife or a favorite walking stick; i.e., something valued that you have with you most of the time. So? Just 'cause I thought you'd like to know, and to introduce wallets as an object of interest.

Before I get into why wallets are of such consuming interest, allow me to offer credit for the following idea to Robert Fulghum, who wrote about wallets in his book, *Maybe, maybe not . . .*

I met recently with a group of thirty educators and mental health practitioners preliminary to a day's adventure curriculum training. Seated in a smallish room, they were waiting for me to drop a few pearls of experiential wisdom on them. What I did ask them to do (absolutely pearl-less, but of some value nonetheless) was take out their wallet (from purse or pocket), and spread the contents on their lap, then share the credit cards, discount slips, photos, ten-punch-holes-and-you-get-a-free *?* card, tokens, receipts, etc., with the people nearest to them.

Before I asked the group to disclose their most personal pocket contents I thought it only fair to share the contents of mine. I'm a minimalist when it comes to wallets. I don't like to carry one, but what are you going to do? And don't talk to me about wearing one around

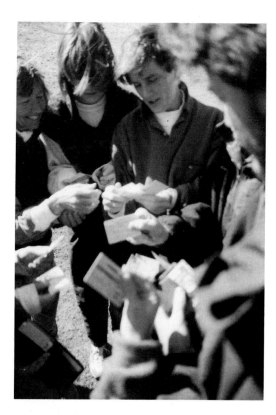

let the latex land mines drop conspicuously to the floor then unabashedly
restashed them within the folds. Anything they had in their wallets paled in
comparison . . .

Within sixty seconds of reaching for
their wallets the level of sharing and
laughter was impressive. During that
first five minutes, the program and I
ceased to exist, as comments like, "You
won't believe this . . ." and, "I had completely forgotten about that . . ." were
shared and humorously appreciated.

Well folded and faded items of note:

- an antique photograph of a young
  girl that the owner *thinks* may be
  a relative.

- a husband's birth announcement
  that a woman had been carrying in
  her various wallets for over 30 years.

- a photograph of an infant that the
  carrier could not identify.

- the most common item (other than
  driver's license and credit cards)
  was the multiple punch or stamp
  cards that give you a free sandwich
  or coffee after you have spent big
  bucks at *that* store. This is obviously a marketing ploy that works.

my neck, that's not negotiable. Wear a
fanny pack (don't call it a *fanny* pack
in Australia, mate) or one of those
blobby sacs that hang just below your
belly? Not likely. Carry a purse? Nope,
I'm a hands free guy. So I put up with a
wallet, and carry only what's absolutely
necessary and needed. However, in
anticipation of asking the group to bare
their credit cards and God knows what
all, I thought it necessary to break a
little ice, so I folded half a dozen condoms
into my billfold. As I talked my way
around a boring Visa card (Exp. date
9/96, whoops!) and driver's license, I

This is a winner folks, Robert F. knew
of what he was suggesting. I have used
wallet sharing as a program opener with
people who had never met, and also
during sessions with participants who
had known each other for years; both
worked, take your pick.

A PREVENTABLE ACCIDENT (BB)

I would be oozing hubris if I told you that I could predict accidents, but I can predict this: if you facilitate the *Trust Fall* exercise over a long enough period of time, one or more of the catchers is going to get clobbered in the face by a faller's elbows, hands, fists, etc. This will result in broken teeth, noses, maxillary arches, bruises, blood, and a severe reduction of trust; unfortunately all the above have happened.

I wrote about this spotting problem in **The Bottomless Baggie**, but that book is now out of print and apparently many of the readers didn't take me seriously, so here it is again.

I am writing this specifically for experienced facilitators; i.e., those people who have already viewed one or more of the sanguinary forays mentioned above and wondered what could have been done to prevent that accident. If you're just starting out in adventure education, yield to experience and trust me, this is not speculation.

Having the faller grab their pants to prevent flailing their arms on descent is worthless, as is putting their hands in their pockets (unless the faller, usually female, is wearing fashionably tight jeans.) Crossing hands, intertwining fingers and rotating the hands up toward the face is good preliminary positioning for a couple adventure stunts, but will accomplish little to keep those hands and elbows from "flapping" on the way down. (See photo) This is

your favorite trust fall position, right? No accidents so far? Try positioning your hands that way, then imagine yourself falling backward and *whip those hands out.* The intertwined hands didn't help much did they?

Rubber deck tennis rings (Yeah, the same kind you use for *Italian Golf* or *Ultimate Deck Tennis—UDT*), will keep "your hands to yourself" without fail. Take one of these colorful rubber pessary-like play objects and slip it over your hands and onto your wrists just before your planned plunge. Hands slip in and out easily, but if you try to remove them rapidly or forcefully, nada happens. It's kind of like an automobile air bag, it stops you, then deflates

for bodily damage, then admonish, "I told you so", because you did.

Over the years I have personally seen at least half a dozen good whacks delivered by flailing fallers. Two of those whacks were hard enough to cause broken noses. Since I started using the rubber rings about five years ago I have not experienced one physical problem caused by flapping arms.

Credit this excellent idea to Ken Demas, a teacher at the Hommocks Middle School in Mamaroneck, NY: runner-up middle school *teacher of the year* in 1994, and all-around nice guy.

RING AROUND THE TRUST

immediately. The ring keeps your hands together for the fall, and can be quickly removed after the fall.

If you or a faller has small hands, you *can* spontaneously slip them out of a single ring during a fall. Try forcing one ring perpendicularly into the center of another ring. This ring-in-a-ring arrangement provides two smaller orifices for two smaller hands. (See photo above)

If a faller is upset or concerned about the idea of having their hands restricted in any way, don't use the rings. But if that person whacks someone in the chops, respond compassionately, check

I had this idea about 17 minutes ago, so here it is fresh off the hypothalamus, or somewhere around there. It's a variation of a couple circular inclinations, but what else can you expect from the windmills of my mind.

Ask your large group to form a circle. I forgot to tell you, this is for large (50+ people) groups standing in a circle. People circles are hard to avoid, don't fight it. Ask the group to count off like this: 1-2, 1-2, 1-2, 1-2-**3**, 1-2, 1-2, 1-2, 1-2-**3**, 1-2 etc. At the end of the circle count, if you happen to end up with an extra 1 or 2 or 3, s'OK, no problem.

Ask the 1's to take one giant step toward the center of the circle, and the 2's and 3's to remain in position, which immediately produces two concentric people circles. Since this is what you want, we're lookin' good. Indicate that people should be facing people; i.e., vis-a-vis, circle to circle.

Remember the *Trust Wave*, (**Quick-Silver**, pg. 234)? No? Well, it's just a matter of having two lines facing one another with all arms are extended toward a person in the other line, so that hands extend a few inches past one another. Then a volunteer walks the length of this "armed" pathway trusting that all hands and arms (at about eye level) will be swept upward as they pass by, narrowly missing their prognathous physiognomy.

The circular people column that you so efficiently put in place above, provides an infinite walking column for the *Trust Wave*. Wow, what a great idea for large groups! My sentiments exactly.

SMALL WORLD CONNECTIONS

Old friend, Charlie Harrington, gave me a small, battery operated "world" for Christmas that plays "It's a Small World After All" as long as you make body (flesh), contact with the two exposed

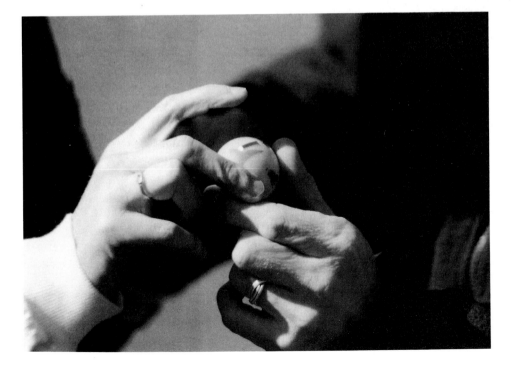

battery terminals. Kind of a neat little toy that loses its appeal about as fast as your wanting to hear "It's a Small World After All" umpteen times. But Charlie, recognizing my limited attention span, suggested that I use it as a demonstration for a workshop group to show that connectedness requires touching. The concept's a little weak but the demonstration is so effective that you can make up your own rationale. Suggest that you are simply demonstrating that the spark of life flows through us all, or some such existential hyperbole.

The demonstration: Ask someone to touch one of the terminals—no gloves. Hold that person's hand. Then you touch the other terminal. If the batteries are strong the song will play conspicuously. If you break grip with that person, the song stops. It's immediately obvious that some kind of electrical current is flowing through or over your bodies. Really, it is!

Begin to add people in a long chain of hand holders and ask the two people at the ends of the line to make contact with the "small world". The tinny machine-like notes of "Small World . . ." begin again.

I've tried this successfully with 40+ connected people. Is there a point of diminishing returns? Is there a measurable time lapse between touching the terminals and hearing the song? Could this device be sold as a weight loss mechanism? Would the electricity travel through a conference group of over 1,000? Does a chicken have lips?

The "World Energy Ball" is sold by Natural Wonders for about 5 bucks.

CHAOS IS THE NORM OR NORMATIVE CHAOS

The following is a name game, in case you get lost.

Sitting in a circle, around a table (if the table is rectangular that's sitting *asquare a table*) or wherever you happen to be, even standing—say your first name, and then say it again, and again and . . . Say it loud, say it soft, gesticulate as you say it, make eye contact as you distinctly pronounce each syllable, say it to the person next to you, across the table. Add some words to what you say, but make your name the center of the statement. "Hi guys, I'm, KARL; That's me, KARL with a **K**; Karl, Karl, Karl . . . Big KARL, little Karl; has a nice ring don't you think?"

After you hear a few other names, use their name in a statement or repeat it, or wink at them and say their name. "Hi Jessie, glad you're here. I'm Karl and you're Jessie. Bill, you're lookin' good today." Jessie, don't forget me, I'm Karl!

If what they say is true, that your own name is the sweetest sound in the world, then say it 'til it cloys. Let other people identify you as the person that is identifying themselves.

There should be names tumbling over names. Don't take turns; don't be rude but don't be too polite either. Pummel each other with names.

Get up and change chairs with someone that you have just made eye contact with, and with whom you have shared names.

If you are moving from one location to another, walking there together allows beau coup time for using names.

Movement, smiles, winks, eye contact, shaking hands, nodding heads, names, names, names . . . It works.

THE SPOTTING GAUNTLET

After the group has tried Willow-in-the-Wind, Levitation, and have experienced

Photo by Nicki Hall

some hands-on falling practice, "lay down the gauntlet" and see if they can make it through *The Spotting Gauntlet* unscathed. Actually it's not that big-a-deal, but perceived challenge, as we know, is often just as good as the real thing.

Ask your group to make two flanking lines facing one another. Distance apart? If the lines reached out toward one another their finger tips would touch.

Explain that you (right . . . YOU, I've done this before, it's your turn) are going to slowly walk between the two lines, then without warning and more than once, fall either right, left, forward or backward. It is up to the two lines; i.e., the group, to keep you from hitting the turf. This is *real* spotting practice.

Since you are to be the first wobbly walker, don't make any radical falling moves that are going to hurt someone, you or them. Test the metaphorical waters before you try your spectacular "fake-'em-out-backward fall".

Encourage people in the group to try the gauntlet, but remember it's *Challenge By Choice*. Discourage peer pressure and individual coersion.

STUNTS

5+5+5 = 550?

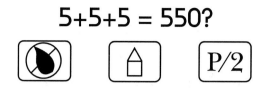

OK, OK . . . this is a little weak, but Hey . . . what the heck, it's taking up less than half a page, and it fits nicely into the Mastermind file of no-prop things to do.

So what's the problem? Look at the title above, and using one straight line, how can you make the equation correct.

And the answer is . . . (Sorry, it's too much hassle to put the answer on the last page.) If you don't want the answer right now just don't look at the next paragraph; turn the page—**NOW!** Whoops too late, you looked.

Draw a straight oblique line on the left hand side of the first plus sign, changing the + to a 4. The equation then reads 545 + 5 = 550. Correct-a-mundo!

COREOLIS/SILOEROC

Stick out your index finger as if you were pointing at something. Hold that pointy hand above your head and begin air-scribing a descending *counterclockwise* spiral with that finger. Let your hand descend slowly, continuing to spiral as your finger descends past your face and on down below your chest. What is the rotational direction of that

diligent digit now? Clockwise? How did that happen? What direction does the water spiral down the drain in your hemisphere? What *is* the meaning of life?

Use this simple self-demonstration as an example of how things change depending upon how you look at the situation. I observed Dave Moriah and his daughter Kira demonstrating this change-of-perception trick at an AEE (Association of Experiential Education) conference session.

One morning you meet a normal looking person who says that she is the world's shortest giant. That afternoon you meet the same person with the confusing announcement that she is also the world's tallest midget. Which is she? It's all in your point of view I'd say—unless she sits on you and really *is* a giant. Sometimes giants are hard to figure out.

Is the previous paragraph a non sequitur of profound proportions or just another fun filled fractious foray in fragmented alliteration?

DUCT (DUCK) TAPE

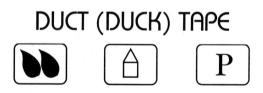

Did you know there is a type of duct tape on the market labeled *Duck* Tape? I did not know that until recently. Neat-o, whimsical to a fault.

I assume that you have, at some point in your life/career, used duct tape to fix or affix something. There are

some commercial products, it seems, that most people have invariably had some previous use for, or contact with. Examples: Quaker's Oats, Kleenex, 3-In-One oil, WD-40, Kool-Aid, etc. Duct tape is definitely one of those products, because what do you think of when a ventilation pipe needs patching, or a canoe springs a leak, or your convertible cover develops a tear, or your blue/gray Honda Accord begins to show rust from the exces-sive amount of salt that they spread all over New England roads *every* time it snows or sleets, which is just about *every* winter week end, and

sometimes well into spring, etc., etc.

But there are also less pragmatic uses for this ubiquitous gray tape and one of them represents what the photos depict, taping healthy, full sized adults to a wall. Why? Come ON! Why not?

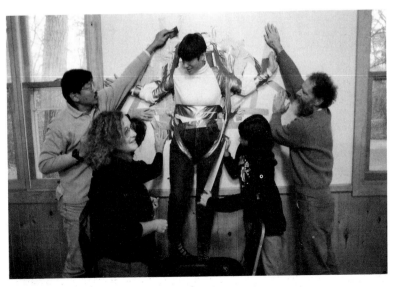

There doesn't have to be a reason. Doesn't duct-taping a person to a wall sound intriguing, almost irresistible? If not, perhaps you had best turn the pages in search for something of a more arcane/mundane bent, because I'm about to tell you how to get started in this bizarre anti-gravity sticky ploy.

It will take less than a roll of 2" duct tape to support a 175 lb. person off-the-wall in the vertical mode. If you are really into serious duct support technology, count on two rolls to support a similar sized person on the ceiling. But since we are just getting started, stick with the wall support scenario. (That was a pun . . . but you didn't get it, did you? You have to be open to these things; stay with me.)

Before beginning, firmly press a six inch length of duct tape to a section of chosen wall that is not viewable by the casual passerby, like behind a couch, then jerk it off in one swipe. This surreptitious tape work is to preclude any problems with spontaneously peeling paint. If sections of paint are ripped off the wall and you decide to continue, consequentially speaking you're on your own, and I told you so; that's my CYA disclaimer for the day.

Ask your tapee to stand on a folding chair or wooden box next to the chosen section of wall so that their weight will be supported during the taping process. Indicate that your volunteer should wear a long sleeve shirt and long pants. Duct tape adheres viciously to hairy parts of the anatomy, as experienced by sorry sun bathers who have opted for a "duct job" rather than the comparatively painless wax-job available at various masochistic cosmetic centers. Am I kidding? Well, who wouldn't. Nevertheless, it is well known in many cultures that the hirsute person does not rest well swathed in duct tape.

Resist offering hints about how to or where to apply the tape. Remember, this is an initiative problem and the solution is up to the group. But I can't help offering a couple suggestions so that during your first tape session you can smile knowingly about what's going on.

I think you will find that a few sections of "duck" reeved through the crotch area and taped obliquely to the wall (approx. 70° up) will help both in total support and comfort. Actually the comfort aspect isn't all that important unless, for some reason, you plan to leave the taped person there for some time. Taped stirrups applied to the feet are also highly effective.

Most people would rather be taped to the wall facing out, but considering the *Challenge By Choice* aspect of this unique manifestation of wall art, don't forget to ask.

When you and the tapee feel that all has been done that needs to be done, gently but with elan, whisk the support chair away and join in the well received and deserved applause. Photographs and beverages are appropriate at this time.

Considerations

- If one roll/one person is getting old, try the one roll/two people taping challenge. Same rules, but all you get is one roll of tape for two chosen participants.

- You may find it useful to require that a male and female be chosen, otherwise two small females are invariably designated as the ob-jectified "volunteers".

- As facilitator, check in occasionally with the people being taped to the wall and inquite about their com-fort and sense of personal space.

- Provide decent spotting for the two tape-hangers when you decide to remove the chairs, as this double challenge is more apt to respond to gravity's call.

- It *is* possible to tape three people to the wall with one roll of tape.

- Take notes of what is being said and done during the taping pro-cess for the group's post-tape review session.

DIVER'S DILEMMA (BB)

Here's some hard skills information that I'm sure will be of consuming interest to every Pamper Pole/Plank veteran who's wondering, what's next?

I was talking recently with Tom Quinn, a Project Adventure trainer who teaches at Cortland SUNY, and who is also their springboard diving coach. Since I have missed my last few 360° spinning attempts at the Pamper Pole trapeze, I asked Tom about the mechanics of a twisting dive and he passed along this valuable bit of information. (What a relief, I thought it was age catching up to me when it was just a botch of body kinetics.)

Tom suggests that when you dive for the trapeze, *don't start the twist until you have completely launched yourself toward the target*; i.e., the twist begins *after* the dive starts. Of course . . . !

Location — PA Adventure Training workshop in the Portland, OR area. The workshop group (and me), were staying in a conveniently located motel that boasted an indoor pool and jacuzzi. As motels go it was just okay, but I really liked the jacuzzi, particularly after a hard day's play. As it turned out we set a workshop world record for inserting 13 people simultaneously into that hot tub. If you have never had the opportunity to participate in a hot tub mob scene, I'd like to pass along a caveat. When everyone removes their broiled bods from the tub there's very little water left causing the jet stream bubblers to blow hot air—kinda like some people I know.

But that most interesting world record vignette was not why I wanted to mention the motel pool venue. In anticipation of diving for the Pamper Pole trapeze later in the week, some of the participants requested a practice body-launch scenario in the pool. Thus, in keeping with PA's exhortation to be creative, we took the life-saving body hook off the wall (the long handled

hook-ended device that's practically never used, but looks good and fulfills insurance requirements), and held the handle an appropriate height and distance above the water to simulate the PP trapeze challenge.

Various dives were made from the side of the pool, and were greeted with spontaneous and wildly exaggerated scores, also punctuated with gleeful shouts of approval from the also-wet sideline judges. Needless to say, all those pool guests not associated with our "party" had long since disappeared. Was this the *horse play* listed as #7 on the long list of "don't dos"? I assume it was, but we were on a quest.

The straight dives were usually successful, and the hand-held pole, with an ersatz trapeze not so firmly attached, was fairly and solidly grabbed. But when a few of the divers, responding to a subtle challenge from the instructional staff, tried a 360° spin toward the trapeze, their efforts were universally awkward and belly-floppish; no one came close to grabbing the bar. After some practice and well intentioned tips, the twisting leaps improved (the scores

remained abysmally low however) but our diver's confidence was being creatively bolstered for the *real thing*.

As it turned out, the newly constructed trapeze bar on the ropes course had been hung so far away from the Pamper Pole that participants were even having trouble making hand/bar contact with a straight dive. Adding a twist to an already impossible dive required a ludicrous display of trust, which a few of the twisted participants ludicrously displayed, and were immediately rewarded with a visual fast-forward North-East-South-West view (if they kept their eyes open) of the entire pole/trapeze scene. Definitely an experiential . . . have you ever, of note.

Being the nice guy that he is, dedicated to diving, adventure programming, and after-hours bridge rappelling, I'm sure that Tom would be happy to detail a practice routine for you that would insure at least a satisfying attempt at a 360° trapeze dive. He can be reached at Cortland SUNY, Attention: Diving Venue. Thanks Tom . . .

> While I'm thinking of it, have you ever wondered . . . if ALL the mosquitoes in the world flew into the Rose Bowl, would they fill it up? I mean . . . right to the brim. What do you think? I still haven't made up my mind, but I'm leaning toward an overflow answer. Wow, would that be a S.L. of mosquitoes, or what?

SWINGING RING

The first "swinging ring" I experienced was at Dartmouth's Moosilauke Lodge in New Hampshire. A ring arrangement had been set up on the rustic porch of the lodge for down-time entertainment, which seemed most of the time. Since then I have seen and heard about many other similar swinging rings, most of the time in a bar/bistro environment. But don't let that juxtaposition turn you off to the recreational value of this just-one-more-try home-made toy.

I doubt that I would be writing this if the Swinging Ring were simply a diversionary time user, but I have found that the inherent challenge of the ring, so obvious to on-lookers, applies well to ropes course use. Students who are looking for something to do or try that is both safe and interesting can involve

themselves in the Swinging Ring challenge while their adventure mates are involved in a bottle neck high element. Whatever the rationale, the Ring set up is not hard to fabricate, and if it doesn't seem to catch on at your ropes site, take it home for the next family barbecue.

You need: one rubber deck tennis ring; one scew-end hook used for hanging bicycles, one small eye screw, approximately 25' of #4 nylon cord (or whatever string you have lying around), and a tree or rustic porch.

I'm going to let the close up photo above tell the story about how to set up the Swinging Ring "catch" area. The "picture" is worth at least 100 words in this case.

Just in case you don't know what this is all about or what you are trying to accomplish: standing approximately opposite the hook and about 15 feet away, *try to swing the string supported ring onto the hook in the least number of attempts.*

Set Up Tips

- The higher you set the eye screw the more gentle the arc of the ring. Also, the higher the set, the longer the string.

- Look for a limb coming off the support trunk that is about 15' high. Set the eye screw in this limb.

- The hook (photo above) should be screwed into the support structure at about chest level, with the hook oriented so that the ring can be captured by the hook. This "capture" is also a function of string length.

- Beware, this activity is insidiously infectious and frustrating.

TRACKING

When was the last time that you walked on a railroad track? Not on the ties, on top of the track. If it has been awhile you better get into a balance mode and find a track to hop onto before the ole iron horse chugs off into the anachronistic sunset.

When I was a kid I loved hanging around RR tracks. I liked the "tracks" area because that's where you found the *best* stones for throwing. As it turned out, I threw the javelin in college and I'm sure most of that arm whip came from hurling and chucking rocks (rocks, not stones; stones are smooth), at tin cans, bottles, milk weed plants or anything else that was silhouetted near the tracks or was unwise enough to move.

And, of course, the "tracks" are where spikes come from. It was necessary for boys to collect rail road spikes. I don't know why, but I know for sure that any loose spike had to be picked up, hefted, maybe even cleaned up a bit

and added to a weighty collection that was vaguely important.

Pennies on the track! Who hasn't lined up pennies along a track and either waited for the 9:17 express, or come back the next day to check out the predictable flattening capability of

tons of rolling steel. How about putting a dime on a penny to see if one can be flattened into the other. Well, can it? It's something you're just going to have to check out on your own.

But the best thing about tracks (you knew this was coming) was to walk 'em. It was like someone had come along and laid a challenge at your feet, not just a little five-and-dime challenge, this one was big, heavy, long and redolent of tar, oil and creosote. How far could you go without falling off? How far could you walk backward, or with your eyes closed?

If you practice walking tracks (I do) there is a centered feeling that is quite unexplainable, a feeling that allows you to walk in a normal manner along the track without flailing arms and flying feet. I walked a mile of track one day in

Georgia and could have continued a lot further if I'd set a goal beyond the mile mark. Walking tracks is one of the best concentration, relaxation exercises I've ever tried; it's like meditating on the move.

If you are "tracking" with a friend, walk the tracks side by side and share some conversation. If you slip off just hop back on. Try reaching out and touching fingers. You will find that even the lightest touch increases the shared balanced feeling considerably.

I've never done much cold weather track walking because I suspect the steel rails would be too slippery, besides it's much more difficult to warm up your throwing arm during cold weather.

Walking the rails isn't a program thing, it's just something to do with a friend occasionally or by yourself anytime. Railroad tracks are a gift.

ROPES COURSE CONSTRUCTION AND IMPLEMENTATION

THE BRASS RING

Is it just a function of age that makes this idea seems significant? You know what a brass ring* is, right? And, if someone grabs a brass ring that means something, correct? I hope so, because what I am about to pass along isn't going to be impressive otherwise.

I was playing some games in Texas a couple weeks ago with a like-minded group of people. (Did you folks know that part of my occupation is playing games? Sorry, of course you know, you bought the book. But if you're just perusing the book, welcome, and it's true, I'm a professional play person. So don't worry I've had experience with this kind of thing, you're in good hands; I take my fun seriously.)

While in Austin, I stayed overnight at Bobby Todd's place, another "older" guy who refuses to grow up. Actually he lives in Dripping Springs, but . . . Bobby is a full time ropes course builder (His incorporated business name is, *Rope Works, Inc.*) and he's one of an unfortunately diminishing breed of buckeroos (Hey, this is TEXAS!) who are willing to share ideas. The following idea is a Todd original, and in my less than humble opinion, a good one. But first let me fill you in on the *Pamper Pole* scene.

There's been some controversy over the last couple years about the incidence of shoulder injury while diving to a trapeze from the *Pamper Pole*. Injury

usually results from poor placement of the trapeze in relation to the jumper's position; i.e., the trapeze is situated too low. If the trapeze is hung low, say about the height of the jumper's waist, the downward force of the dive puts an inordinate amount of kinetic pressure on the individual's arms and shoulders. This downward dive in combination with the pendulum whipping action of the lower part of the body can result in shoulder injury, particularly if the jumper has a strong grip and attempts to grab the bar with only one hand

The obvious solution is to change the height of the trapeze; it should be at least eye level to the jumper. But if your potential jumpers are still choosing not to challenge themselves, other whimsical solutions are available.

Some adventure centers with a keen sense of go-for-it humor use a rubber chicken as the diving goal. The dangling chicken is held in position by a length of #4 nylon cord (around its neck of course). The cord leads from the chicken through a small hardware store pulley on the overhead cable to the ground. A designated "chicken holder" on the ground lightly grips the cord holding the faux fowl in position. When the diver (me in the photo below) grabs the chicken, the cord holder lets go, allowing the daunting duo to descend together. The climber is then heaped with fowl accolades and the chicken is unceremoniously hauled up for the next grab-and-go. (The photo was taken at the annual T.E.A.M. Conference at Northeastern Illinois University in Chicago.)

---

* *Brass ring* on a merry-go-round. Still no flicker of recognition? Sorry, you're going to have to ask your parents.

they grab it, to descend with it and take home the souvenir of a substantial commitment. Here's the scenario that Bobby passed along to me.

Purchase a 24" long, small boat, plastic, air-filled bumper (about five bucks at Wal-Mart). Each end will have an integral eye built into the float for rope attachment. With a sharp knife cut a slice directly on-end though this eye. Shove a small diameter brass ring through this slice and into the eye.

The brass ring itself is about 1/8" in diameter, with a 5" interior diameter. I found a similar brass ring recently in the hobby section (again at Wal-Mart), for 38 cents. Suspend this float/ring arrangement using a section of #4 cord, as per the chicken scenario above.

When the jumper grabs the ring it detaches easily from the eye through the cut area. Make sure the word *easily* applies to this brass ring detachment, otherwise finger injury could result.

The haul cord system mentioned above for use with the rubber chicken also applies to the replacement of a brass ring after a successful "catch"; i.e., lower the float and insert another ring.

I was thinking that if you could find a company that sells plastic "brass" rings, you could have your company name either silk screened or embossed on the

Or, try diving to simply ring a suspended bell. Remember to suspend the bell from something other than the belay cable. If the bell is connected directly to the belay cable, tintinnabulation will manifest itself as more than just an onomatopoetic choice of words. *If you don't want to look up the words, don't bother, it's just me entertaining myself.*

Or (finally Bobby's idea), allow the participant to dive for a brass ring and if

ring. Then your clientele takes home not only a valued souvenir of a substantial accomplishment, but also a piece of displayed advertisement. Buy low—sell high.

SERVING SLEEVES

It just doesn't seem right to say this but, **I've stopped using serving sleeves** (SS). So you're thinking, "what the heck is a serving sleeve?" If you're not into ropes course construction, these next few paragraphs won't hold much interest.

A serving sleeve is a no-moving-parts piece of galvanized metal that serves to crimp the working end of the cable

back onto it's standing part. (Now you're REALLY not interested.) It's function is to keep the working end of the cable from fraying and puncturing skin. SS's are lightweight, will not rust and are fairly easy to install.

A serving sleeve's main drawback is that once installed (squeezed into place with a vice-grip tool) it's difficult to remove from the cable. If it's necessary to retighten a cable, it will also be necessary to remove the SS; as I mentioned, a real pain. The aggravation occurs when an installed SS detaches from its crimped position due to heavy foot traffic and then, because it has been crimped so tightly, maintains its position on the single cable, tinkling up and down its length until someone, out of frustration, *tapes it* into position near the cable clamp connection.

So now all I do is what was done years ago before we discovered serving sleeves. I secure the working end of the cable to the standing part with multiple wraps of plastic electrician's tape. The tape will hold the cable together for years and it's easy to remove with a knife if the cable needs adjusting. Tape

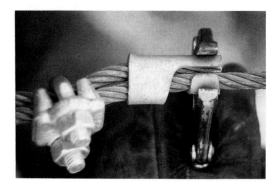

is also faster and easier to apply than installing a SS, less expensive too.

Caveats: #1— Black tape does not wrap or adhere well at below or near freezing temperatures. #2 — If you install enough SS's with a vice grip you *will* get an impressive blood blister in the soft tissure between your thumb and index finger. (Photo not included, but I've got a great one that would look good in any medical journal.)

I know there are techniques for removing a SS that involve two pairs of vice grips rotated in opposite direction, and that there is even a specific tool designed for this purpose, but what's the use? The tape works and until somebody shows me a device (it will probably be plastic) that applies on and comes off easily, I'll continue serving the sleeve with black tape.

PORTABLE PAMPER POLE

You've got to be kidding! A portable PAMPER POLE? That's off the wall. Too true! Off the ground actually, and here's how . . .

What You Need

- A 16–20 foot 4×4 board with minimum knots—pressure treated or not; doesn't matter.

- About 8 - 3/8" staples and 4 - 1/2" staples, or a dozen modular climbing blocks. You can also alternate use of staples and blocks.

- A hard rubber 4×4 pad (like the ones used on a zip-brake block). Use of this pad is only necessary if you plan to use the pole exclusively indoors.

- An overhead belay point location that is at least 25–30' high.

Preparation

- Rout (bevel) the edges and corners of the 4×4.

- Sand the surface of the board with #100 grit sandpaper, making sure all potential splinters are removed.

- Using Sikaflex adhesive, secure the 4×4 rubber pad to what will eventually be the base of the pole. Score the rubber surface with a knife before applying the adhesive.

- Screw a 10" × 10" square section of 3/4" plywood to the other end of the 4×4 board. Pre-drill and countersink the plywood, then use five — 3" flat-topped galvanized wood screws to secure the platform to the top of the 4×4. Squeeze on a dollop of Sikaflex or Elmer's adhesive before you secure the screws. Bevel and sand all edges of the plywood platform. (I have to admit that simply nailing the plywood platform to the top of the

4×4 functions just as well and is a lot easier. But I'm obliged to offer the screwed-n-glued technique for those handy folks who like to "do things right".)

- Install the blocks or staples (pre-drill with a 1/4" bit for the 3/8" staples, and a 7/16" bit for the 1/2" staples) to produce a challenging climb. Alternate the use of staples and blocks.

- If you use fiberglass holds, grind off whatever portion of the block extends beyond the edge of the 4×4; mostly an aesthetic thing.

Procedure

Ask 4–6 committed participants to manually support the pole vertically, directly below the chosen belay point. Helmet/Climber? Yes.

A *belayed* student attempts to climb the hand-held pole, then either sits on top, does a Shamu (belly down on the platform), or most impressively stands vertically without help from the belay rope. Gaining the top of the platform completes the challenge. A lateral dive from this position to a trapeze is unrealistic and will cause the pole to shift forcefully from vertical; it's an "equal and opposite reaction" thing.

To promote an initiative flavor to the attempt, make available four 30 foot sections of 1/2" multiline or slash sections of climbing rope. The object is to support the pole during a climb using the rope. Where to tie on the ropes? Where to stand? What knot to use? How to communicate with the climber? Somebody might have to say something or offer an idea.

As an additional challenge, suggest that the holders and climbers first communicate, then see how far the pole can be tilted while the climber attempts to maintain a balanced vertical posture on the platform. Use a minimum of six holders for this balance stunt.

Twenty feet is about the longest 4×4 you will find at a lumber yard, and even that length will have to be custom ordered. A longer climbing "pole" (25'+) can be easily fabricated by bolting on two shorter parallel sections of 4×4 to the bottom sides of that 20 footer.

TRYING-TO-DESTRUCT TESTING

How many "falls" can an 11mm kern-mantle climbing rope sustain as used in a typical sling-shot belay ropes course set up? When should I retire my Pamper Pole belay rope? How many years can I keep a ropes course belay rope in use? And the definitive answer is—nobody knows.

Somewhat definitive answers have been shared around the industry for years and an amalgam of answers have been repeated over and over until various conservative answers have been created and assimilated as standards. The answer you hear stated with the most conviction by the most respected authority is the one usually accepted. "You may use climbing rope for two

years on a ropes course, or one year in the case of *Pamper Pole* belay use, and then it must be retired." Bases covered, lots of new rope sold.

About five years ago, at the Project Adventure site in Hamilton, MA, I set up a simulated ropes course test fall situation to determine how many falls an 11mm rope could sustain in a simulated ropes course belay set up before breaking. After about 30 falls the rope, pulleys and carabiners were stolen from the testing site; end of test.

During the winter months, for the last two years, I have served as teacher-in-residence at Georgia College in Milledgeville, GA. One of my responsibilities, other than teaching, is to work on the ropes course (new events and maintenance). During the winter of 1996, Jim Wall (Director of the Outdoor Center) and I decided it would be useful to the industry to re-establish the test abandoned years ago in Massachusetts. We were also personally interested in the results, and both intuitively guessed what the outcome would be.

Please recognize that this test and the one that follows were not scientifically conducted and should be used only as an indication that the safety gear used on a ropes course is well engineered for the tasks assigned.

The test was set up as follows:

- The test object to be dropped was a cast-off cast iron heating unit that weighed 175 lbs. We chose that weight because it came close to the UIAA drop test mass used for establishing a climbing rope fall rating.

- The anchor point was a 4' section of utility pole (dead-man) buried near the plumb line of the drop weight. A doubled section of 1/2" multiline was passed around the dead-man and tied with a double fisherman's knot. Approximately 9" of rope extended above the ground. Two non-locking carabiners connected one end of the climbing rope to this in-ground rope anchor.

- A three pulley haul arrangement was established that allowed a 2:1 mechanical advantage for lifting the 175 lb. weight.

- The weight was dropped an average of 10 feet each time. This distance was not precise because

the test rope stretched considerably after a few falls, in fact so much so that a hole had to be dug directly below the weight to preclude the test weight hitting the ground. The hole was established rather than having to untie and retie the test rope.

- The support trees were approximately 18" in diameter at the belay cable connection point, which was located 25 feet above ground level.

- The 3/8" belay cable length measured 18'6" between support trees, with a drape of approximately 21" when the 175 lb. weight was statically applied.

- A bowline-on-a-bight was tied at one end of the test rope, with a figure eight loop established at the other end.

Observations

- The belay rope did not break after *600 dynamic falls.*

- The bowline knot untied easily at the end of the test drops. The figure eight loop was hopelessly jammed.

- Considering the ten foot falling distance as an average, the test weight fell over 1.3 miles during the testing.

- The steel rapid link supporting the S/S shear reduction pulley distorted the aluminum of the pulley cheeks (clip-in orifice) to the extent that the pulley would have been retired during a safety inspection.

The engineering and construction of the test site was accomplished with the help of: Dave Klim, Sam Little, Craig Dinn, and Jim Wall. Many other Georgia College staff and students applied their muscle during the very physical (and social), pull and drop sessions.

An additional destructive test that we conducted at Georgia College might also be of interest; strength of an eye splice as per the number of tucks made.

I've read in various catalogs and technical publications over the years that three tucks in natural fiber rope and five tucks in synthetic rope produce an eye splice that is 95% of the tensile strength of the rope.

In the back of my mind I always wondered if that was correct, but you know how it is, you quote a certain statement often enough and it eventually becomes a personal truism.

So, using practically the same testing set up as reported above, we dropped the 175 lb. weight onto an eye-spliced section of 1/2" synthetic rope. Here's some of the set up and testing facts:

- The double eye-spliced section of rope was approximately 24" long (eye to eye). One eye had *two tucks,* the other eye had five.

- The weight was first simply suspended from the splices (no shock loading); nothing visual happened.

- The 175 lb. weight was dropped approximately 18", three separate times. No distortion of the eye or fiber separation was noticed.

- Using a 6'6" eye-clamped cable extension, the weight was dropped two separate times on the same eye-spliced section of rope. The falling distance was approximately 8' each time. The splice did not come apart, in fact did not even distort. The three cow-tailed ends of the splice were not pulled out of their original position.

I had another section of rope eye-spliced with three tucks, but we never tested it. If I couldn't get two tucks to give way, what's the use?

As the result of this *single* test I'm certainly not suggesting it's a waste of time and rope to do more than two tucks, but it makes you think, and should also make you feel better about the safety margins built into the material and procedures that we regularly use on a ropes course.

SIDE-GRINDER

Some time ago I suggested using an abrasive cutting wheel to cut through cable if your regular cable cutters were non-functional or they were somehow left home on the dining room table. I also suggested that the cutting wheel be attached to your Skil-saw. I'm retracting that recommendation. Don't get me wrong, the wheel does a decent job of cutting the cable, but it does a better job if you buy a tool that goes along with a grinding wheel—the side-grinder.

I probably wouldn't have even mentioned the switch from Skil-saw except for the fact that the side-grinder also does a bang-up job of cutting off protruding 5/8" bolts. You know, all the inevitable threaded-end flesh rippers left over from the many nut eye bolts used on a Mohawk Walk. In the past I'd dread the hack-saw work necessary to trim off all the threaded bolt ends, now a side-grider does the job easily and as a bonus provides a miniature fireworks display.

When you grind, wear safety glasses, a long sleeve shirt and long pants. Don't ignore this suggestion. That sparking pyrotechnic display results from small pieces of hot metal flying off the grinding wheel. If those glowing globules make contact with bare skin or corneas, pain and body damage results. I know you knew that, I'm just being responsible.

VARIATIONS

SCRABBLE VARIATION

The original activity that this variation is based upon is in **FUNN STUFF**; Vol. 1., pg. 41. The stated procedure is to have each person in a group write their name on a black board or on poster paper so that each name is connected by letters to one or more of the other names. Think of a completed Scrabble game and you'll get an approximate visual of what all the connected names in a group should look like. Follow Scrabble rules as names are added unless it becomes obvious that someone is going to be left out because their name won't fit, then do whatever's necessary. *The only rules are the rules that work.*

After the group has produced their own Scrabbled version of representing their names for all to see, ask them (not necessarily right then) to list in smaller print the names that they have been known by in the past, and to draw a line from that list to their "real" name. I grew up with the cognomen Skip, so Skip would be part of my list. My children call me Dad. I was also occasionally referred to as Rohnke/Donkey by some of my dippy elementary classmates (still bothers me!)

Nickname lists may be long or short, but everyone seems to have at least one other name. Keep the original list posted and a felt-tipped pen available so that participants can add to the list when they are ready to commit.

There's obviously some ice breaking going on as a list like this is created and perused by the rest of the group, but perhaps the greatest gain is in the area of trust, trust that you can reveal something private about yourself without fear of being ridiculed. Having said that, it's obvious this exercise needs to be facilitated carefully. Or perhaps the greatest facilitating insight comes from recognizing that your group is not ready for this level of trust yet, and not creating the nickname list all.

BATTER UP! . . . ON THE LADDER

Tim Haynor suggested using baseball bats instead of three foot lengths of one inch diameter dowel to establish the

Human Ladder (**The Bottomless Bag Again !?**, pg. 14). Sounds good to me, but you better have a serious base or soft ball program to pony-up the minimum ten "rungs" necessary to establish a decent ladder. (Don't be too concerned about my reference to minimum number of rungs, I just made that up, 9 rungs work fine, eight-n-a-half isn't so good.)

The *Human Ladder* is established by having two shoulder-to-shoulder flanking lines pair up so that each person in one line is directly facing another person in the other line. A bat is shared between the pairs and held solidly at about waist level so that a volunteer "climber" can walk on top of the bat rungs from one end of the line to the other.

Wood or aluminum? Your choice, but either way some traditionalist is going to be miffed or wiffed, as the case may be.

GROUP JUGGLING VARIATION

You know how it goes; you've been presenting the same initiative problem for years, then BOOM someone mentions a useful variation and you think, "How come I didn't think of that?" Happens all the time.

After you have gone through the basic *Group Juggling* scenario (**Silver Bullets**, pg. 112) distribute one soft throwable object to each player and suggest that they attempt to complete as many simultaneous throws (no drops), as there are people in the group. Cooperation, communication, trust, fun . . . it's all there. Substitute a couple raw eggs to increase the commitment factor.

If you have a largish group, divide them up into smaller sub-groups and ask them to establish a group juggling, person-to-person throwing sequence. After the sequence has been established and memorized, ask the groups to disperse and then reform into smaller circles with different people in the new groupings.

The challenge now is for each individual to throw and receive the ball from their original partners notwithstanding what group they currently find themselves in or where that group is located. Let that last sentence soak in some. After playing classic *Group Juggle* for years it might take a minute or so for this new approach to seem OK, or legal, or possible.

Encourage yelling names or making a distinctive sound when a throw is made.

Lost your balls? Try this variation of *Group Juggling* with no balls-a-tall.

Instead of setting up the sequence by throwing a ball, point to a person across the circle, then that person points to someone else, etc. After the sequence has been set (allow a couple point-to-a-person run-throughs), ask the initial person to walk toward their designated person. The person being walked toward can begin their walk as soon as the person walking toward them has made physical contact. That person then moves out, walking toward their designated person across the circle.

You can set this up as a contest against time or as simply an exercise in efficiency. Just remember who pointed toward you and who you pointed toward as the group established the sequence. All least you don't have to worry about dropping a ball.

TWO VARIATIONS OF MERIT

Phil Ritchie of Elmcrest Hospital in Portland, CT generously offered these inventive variations of two golden oldies.

Traffic Jam

If you have a large group, say 16–24 folks, and want to include everyone in the *Traffic Jam* initiative without setting up two separate problems, simply use the shape of an $\mathbb{X}$ instead of one long line. The same rules apply (*Silver Bullets*, pg. 122), but " . . . the visual presentation adds to creative brainstorming and conflict."

Trolley

Use **three** rope festooned lengths of 4×4 rather than the typical two pieces.

"The new visual presentation adds to the problem solving."

Also, remember that it's only necessary to have ropes on the front and back of the Trolley boards; i.e., a total of four ropes per pair of boards. The people in between the rope holders hold onto one another; makes sense to me.

ACRONYM VARIATION

There is a long list of acronyms and initialisms in FUNN STUFF Vol. #1. Refer to that anthology for this variation of what I had in mind there.

Place acronym cards (nothing fancy, just print the acronym or initialism on a 4×6 card), randomly around a room so that the group or individuals have to circulate and write down (provide pencils and paper), what they think the letters designate. Encourage sharing ideas and comments. Remember, the purpose of doing this is not to memorize a list of acronyms, it is to get people mixing and talking to one another.

Allow a set time, depending upon the number of cards you set out, then have everyone assemble and hold up each collected card for the group to identify. By this time there will be considerable interest in what the acronyms mean, so spend the time necessary to identify the letter sequences. Knowing that LASER stands for *Light Amplification Serialized Emmision of Radiation* will not help anyone on their SAT scores, but it's interesting to know that the letters making up the word mean something. If

this rationale isn't enough, refer to the last sentence in the paragraph above.

It's not necessary to keep score unless someone asks who won, then indicate (sotto voce), that you're pretty sure they did.

HULA HOOP SPIDER'S WEB

Just another winner in the growing pantheon of *Spider Web* variations.

Purchase about 15 hula hoops of three different sizes (two sizes, three, four, all the same size—doesn't really matter, but I feel obligated to be creative *and* definitive sometimes).

Lay the hoops on the ground so that they are all touching one another on their circumferences (all the interior hoops should be "touched" in four places; NESW kind of thing). Using shredded

Photographer Unknown

sections of panty hose or 3/16 bungee cord, tie the hoops together where they touch. Use the quadruple granny knot for this critical attachment.

When your basically rectangular arrangement of circles is complete, attach a short section of 1/4" bungee cord to the four corners (which really aren't corners at all but actually the upper/or lower quadrant of a corner hoop's arc—now that's what I call genuinely confusing.) Check out the photo.

Hang this rectangular arrangement of circles between two conveniently spaced trees, poles, volleyball standards, or Grecian columns. That's it; spider away.

MOHAWK WALK VARIATIONS

Creatively divide the group in half. Ask each half to start from opposite ends of a Mohawk Walk. (The Mohawk Walk is a low ropes course element. If you don't recognize the name or activity you're at kind of a disadvantage here.) Offer each group a rubber ring and indicate that each ring must be eventually transferred to the team coming in the opposite direction, so that the ring ends up back at its starting location.

Rules & Penalties

- If a person carrying a ring falls off (touches the ground), that player must return to the beginning.

- If any other person falls off, they must return only to the cable support they just left.

- The ring must be passed hand-to-hand to the other team; it cannot be thrown.

- The offered "crutch" (a *real* crutch certainly displays a distinctive level of panache, but an appropriate length of dowel or sapling is okay too), can be used to make ground contact anywhere on the traverse, but it must always move forward. Any backward movement results in loss of the crutch. Pivoting movements forward and/or backward on the ground are allowed. The crutch cannot be passed person-to-person in reverse.

Individual crutches are offered to both halves of the team.

BLINDFOLD POLYGON REDUX

I was recently part of a full day environmental get together that involved teachers from many surrounding schools. I was asked by the programmers to tag along on one of the ecology hikes and "suggest a game if the situation seemed right"; here's what resulted.

The trail teacher, who had the primary responsibility to pick the trails and choose interpretive stops, suggested that I think of something interesting for the group to attempt that involved both team building and measuring distances. As the result, he indicated being able to weave that experience into his field lecture on counting trees within a chosen biome.

I asked the group to make a circle and count off by twos; i.e., 1-2, 1-2, etc.

Twos, please step behind a one. Ones, please close your eyes and wait for instructions. Twos, you may talk with your partner (no one else) but you cannot touch that person.

Having previously tied the ends of a 50' rope together (any simple bend will do), I tossed the bundled rope into the center of the half blind circle. All the group had to do was simply retrieve the rope and use it to make a circle, then a triangle. Only the *ones* could touch the rope, only the *twos* could give instructions.

The group numbered about 30. There was much nervous laughter and initial confusion, and finally movement toward retrieving the rope. As soon as some progress was recognized, the *two's* chatter slowed to meaningful

comments and the *ones* began keying in to their assigned voice. All the good stuff that you expect from an initiative problem was being experienced.

Whether this group of mostly female elementary teachers felt bonded as a team as the result of this simple exercise, I'd be reluctant to say, but there was definitely a sense of accomplishment when the triangle was finally completed and viewed by all. They had not learned any technical ways to measure or survey an area, but they were obviously more alert than five minutes earlier, and ready for whatever came next.

I was pleased; the trail teacher looked pleased; the group sounded pleased — way to go Karl! I wonder if you can make a living doing this kind of stuff?

OPINIONS & TIPS

XL* WORKSHOP

The following paragraphs were written some time ago in anticipation of offering an adventure experience to people my age. It was my thinking (still is) that folks in their 50's and 60's would be up for some adventure and fun, but might be initially intimidated if they anticipated having to keep up with a younger generation. Thus the XL idea.

My father, married at 87 (I was his best man) quotes, *"Don't complain about old age, many people are denied it."* At 59, I figure I'm definitely on the downside of middle age and trying not to complain, but it's tough sometimes when there's no doubt that your speed, flexibility, and endurance are not only suspect but undeniably age eroded. It's mildly depressing when taken-for-granted skills and abilities are no longer readily at hand, and when situations demanding physical output have to be "paid for" with bouts of stiffness and longer-than-remembered recuperation time. In fact, it's often easier (mentally & physically) to avoid hard breathing/body-in-motion activities, resulting in all the negative affective and physical scenarios that you have either read about or personally experienced. If you're near 50 or over, I expect you know what I'm talking about.

Looking for the definitive answer? Me too. And I think I'm onto something by suggesting getting together with like-minded individuals (female/male) and experiencing some exciting activities in a safe and supportive experiential atmosphere that's not tea-groupish, embarrassing, or fabricated.

Here's something I want to make available to those folks near or beyond the big Five O. Let's set aside a couple days of fun and excitement for like-minded players looking for a stimulating experience with people near their own age, where the adventure doesn't depend upon exotic travel, expensive gear or above average conditioning. And particularly where the experience isn't dependent upon drugs or alcohol to stimulate group interaction or incentive to participate. (Nothing wrong with a beer or glass of wine at dinner tho'.)

I have been involved with these types of adventure experiences over the past 25 years: i.e., FUNN* clinics emphasizing cooperation, communication and trust within a supportive go-for-it atmosphere. I also feel, if the experience is not enjoyable, no matter how good it is for you, a repeat visit is not in the cards. Fatigue, hunger, loneliness and overt discomfort are useful discipline tools for the armed services, and for which I have no enlistment forms.

Challenge By Choice promises that each participant has the choice to either participate or observe, so that if an offered activity is perceived as a problem, either physically or emotionally, an individual can decide (without the hassle of cajoling or peer pressure) what is most comfortable for them to try at that particular time. There is no pressure to perform, only support for

---

XL — Excellent Living

FUNN — Functional Understanding's Not Necessary

whatever participant decision is made, and an on-going commitment to provide the safest possible experience.

Wouldn't it be a treat to be involved in a series of challenging situations that allow you to flow between active participant and welcomed observer, where the choice and the extent of participation is entirely up to you, AND to be genuinely supported in whatever choice you make? More specifically, here's what I'm suggesting.

The XL Adventure experience would be open to any female or male or couple who has completed 50 ± years of being alive. Since the level of participation is self chosen, there is no upper age limit. The only thing I recommend is not to let the level of anticipated fun blunt your keen and mature sense of what your muscles are going to feel like tomorrow, particularly as you just get out of bed. Remember, even 100% high-test Colombian coffee can only do so much.

Two days and nights of activity involvement that key on playing and adventuring together; which is not to say that I don't enjoy an occasional bike ride or walk alone, but the real joy in adventure I have found is shared. The shared time format offers adventure games, initiative problems, and trust activities that involve individual participation and group sharing.

Have you ever . . .

. . . shared standing on taut cables with 15 other people?

. . . laughed with a group 'til you cried?

. . . trusted a just-met group, physically and emotionally?

. . . learned how to tie a knot just because it looked like fun?

. . . set a world's record with your group?

. . . worked on a group initiative problem that required thinking and physical action?

Have you ever wondered where the proverbial "child within" went, the one that welcomes activities like the ones above? I think I know where he/she is hiding, but these types of things don't show up on X-rays so I'm not surprised at your amazement. Let me show you some simple laugh inducing maneuvers that cause a whimsical squeezing of that hidden recess and a joyful reintroduction to your own good buddy.

I have facilitated a couple of these sessions with excellent response from the participants. If you're interested in the concept, let me know. Let's get a weekend group together and go for it.

TEACHING/FACILITATION

You need to know the difference between teaching and facilitating, more specifically the difference between an adventure teacher vs. an adventure facilitator. The difference in this context has little to do with a dictionary's definition.

Teach — "To cause to know a subject; make to know the disagreeable consequences of some action; guide the studies of . . ."

Facilitate — "To make easier."

words and example. This is not the time to teach.

• . . . offers encouragement, and attempts to keep the group enthusiastically on task. If a teacher/facilitator offers hints and guides the student's interaction, the group loses the opportunity to feel that they cooperatively came up with the answer themselves. Students predictably wait for a teacher to give them answers, because that's what teachers do. Don't!

• . . . subtly observes how the group is working together and mentally sets aside topics for later discussion. This "sit down" discussion time is called synonymously PROCESSING, DEBRIEFING or REVIEWING. Don't let these terms put you off. There is nothing complicated or intimidating about the process of verbally sharing an experience. "Adventuring" without the occasional opportunity for *reviewing* is mostly recreational and precludes much of what can result from a shared experience.

In the context of adventure programming a facilitator (you) is primarily someone who:

• . . . presents an initiative problem to a group, setting the perimeters for safety and operation, *then steps back and lets the group work out the problem themselves.* Teachers are trained to teach, to show how, to guide by

ADVENTURE

Here's a couple definitions for your occupational and personal survival file.

Adventure, in the context of pure adventure, is anything you make of it; i.e., anything that you do associated with risk and excitement where the outcome remains in question. The risk does not necessarily have to be physical and the excitement factor is entirely dependent upon the experience quotient of the individual. Examples include anything you personally experience or conceptu-alize—*anything*. But make no mistake, pure adventure can be deadly if the limits of endurance and capability are pushed.

Programmed adventures are those established and controlled activities used by educators to incite the emo-tions and reactions associated with pure adventure. The risk associated with the chosen task is actually minimal, but the perception of the risk/danger to the participant is real and poignantly felt.

Your occupational survival depends upon understanding the difference between adventure and programmed adventure, particularly if you are creative enough to come up with your own brand of excitement. Having been in that creative curriculum position a number of times, allow me the space for a suggestion. Try whatever your fecund imagination has suggested before you foist your ideas upon an unsuspecting and largely trusting audience. It's necessary (morally and legally) for you to take the lumps and bumps associ-ated with whatever trial and error that's sure to occur.

Be personally adventurous to what-ever extent your skill and practical know-how keep you in the game (of life) but also recognize that pure adventure has no place in an "adventure pro-gram". You had better be sure what the outcome of your chosen adventure activity is going to be, or you're playing with legal fire.

MISCELLANEOUS FUNN

Elevate the Play Quotient

What can you do to create an initial playful atmosphere in a workshop format, particularly with a (young or older) group that has not played for years?

Early on present your sure-fire, grab 'em, opening activities; i.e., those tested playful ploys that are studiously atypical, easy to explain, easy to respond to, and which causes the participants to joyfully anticipate what's coming next. Examples—*Categories*, *Moon Ball*, *Toe Tag*, *Impulse genre*, *Pairs Tag*

Knowing When to Quit or Change Activities or Leave a Venue

Look for fidgeting among the group, also symbolic positioning or posturing as if they were going to leave the circle. Check facial expressions and direction of gaze. Genuine smiles and laughter indicate your still on the right track. Grimaces and darting glances toward their car, sleeping quarters, coffee source; etc., means move on.

If someone is operating a chain saw or lawn mower near the site where you are attempting to lead an activity or discussion, find another area. (I don't know what it is, karma perhaps, but it seems like custodial-type folks follow me around with power tools, ready to fire 'em up whenever I sit a group down for a discussion.) Try not to choose a site that exposes the participants to casual spectating by people passing by.

Being an Effective Adventure Pedagogue

Differentiate between an effective, spontaneous, outrageous approach and a stupid, prepared, fabricated attempt at being spontaneous. This has to do with charisma, an innate sense of timing, experience, and a willingness to occasionally appear the fool. There isn't much difference between a safe approach and using calculated abandon effectively, but the subtle variation makes all the difference in how the students perceive their instructor, and

eventually how effective they will become as facilitators.

Empowerment — Letting Go

Differentiate the fine line between being the center of attention and the ability to empower a group. This requires considerable self confidence and "having your act together". Someone who is still questioning the effectiveness of their own approach, will have trouble empowering a student group.

Practice Before You Preach

Know the rules to the games and activities well, well enough so that your presentation is easy to understand, puts your students at ease (they know that you know what you are talking about) and is entertaining—make it fun.

FACILITATE OR RECREATE?

Instill fun, but amidst the frivolity remember that the established enjoyment factor is your lever to further learning. If your eager and smiling group moves enthusiastically from game, to initiative, to game, etc. without any inclination as to what they are trying to accomplish as a group, you are presenting an entertaining recreation program and not much else.

If you are working in a summer camp program and full-bore recreation is all you want or need, keep up the pace, some good things are bound to happen.

But if you want your audience (elementary to corporate) to experience the benefits of group problem solving, the enjoyment of positive competition, and the individual exhilaration of achieving beyond anticipation, your role as facilitator must eventually be honed and developed to anticipate, motivate and handle the various people-to-people situations that predictably occur, and which closely mirror those typical scenarios that make up our day-to-day existence.

Start off playing for the fun of it, but recognize that once you become a games person there are a plethora of useful insights and learnings that are initially secondary to the fun, but soon become the raison d'être toward achieving your curriculum or bottom-line goals.

IT'S SIMPLER THAN IT SEEMS

About five years ago I collected some thoughts about adventure training and recorded the material represented below. I often refer to this list just before

starting a job or presenting at a conference to remind myself that the basics of
adventure education are not complicated.

Training Truisms

- People are usually capable of
  achieving well beyond their self
  imposed limits.

- Most people are stimulated by
  reasonable risk and challenge. The
  risk or challenge does not have to
  be physical.

- People will try harder when given
  the choice to try, rather than being
  directed or coerced into "trying" —
  Challenge By Choice

- There's more value to failing-
  forward than failing to try.

- Many people have forgotten how to
  play without the crutch of win/lose
  competition.

- The best performers are not necessarily the most effective leaders.

- Students will consistently try, if
  convinced that their teacher/
  mentor is also willing to occasionally share the same risk.

- Trust can be diminished in a much
  shorter time than it takes to establish.

- Effective communication involves
  the pleasant paradox of more
  listening than talking.

- Most fun depends upon funn*.

The following four concepts are
emphasized during adventure training.

1. **Cooperation**—working voluntarily
   together to achieve a goal

2. **Communication**—comfortably
   listening and talking to one
   another

3. **Trust**—emotional and physical

4. **Fun**—spontaneous and
   encompassing

Trying to achieve the first three goals
and have fun at the same time is key,
recognizing that if the participants do
not enjoy what they are doing or learning, they will not return willingly for
more of what you have to offer. Of the
four, FUN is initially the most important.

*FUNN = Functional Understanding's Not
Necessary

MISCELLANEOUS ADVENTURE

CASE OF THE MISSING POWER PACK

A Barn Building Vignette

I used to work alone building ropes courses, partly because I didn't mind doing the work by myself, and during the early years of Project Adventure (before the Inc. was added) there weren't many of us to go around. On one particular job, I had been hired by *The National Technical Institute For The Deaf* to install high and low indoor ropes course elements in a barn, dutifully called **The Red Barn**, because it was. It was February in Rochester, New York and C O L D.

The turned-on folks that had contracted with PA to do the work were eager to insure that the installation would be completed before spring, so I had volunteered (a decision easily made in a warm room in September), to make the trip, because I was intrigued about the uniqueness of installing ropes course elements in a *real* wooden barn.

Plus, as an incentive, I was offered practically *carte blanche* for whatever creative ideas or bizarre inclinations I could come up with; these folks wanted something different.

I don't like cold weather, in fact, I can't think of *anything* I like cold, except maybe ice cream. During the first day of work, the outside temperature was in the teens, and since the barn was unheated, the inside thermometer registered teens also. The protection from wind chill obviously saved my ectomorphic body from frost bite, but the interior of that cavernous barn was not what I'd call comfy. However, with enthusiastic help from one of the deaf students, the work progressed at a comfortable pace, but corporal comfort was definitely out of context, considering my numb fingers, stinging toes, nipped ears, and red nose. . . .

On the morning of the third day at the barn I was again working alone, trying to horse the extension ladder around so I could get to the peak rafter support beam. I needed to drill a hole in that key-stone chunk of wood in order to place a nut eye bolt as a belay anchor. The fully extended ladder was set vertically, with it's top-most section more-or-less jammed between the support beam and the roofing boards. It wobbled some, but seemed reasonably secure.

Since no one was around to help, I fired up their heavy-weight alternator to juice the drill (the top of that ladder was *not* the place to spend time rotating a bit brace) and, supporting all the attachment and shear reduction paraphernalia on my climbing belt, laboriously baby-stepped my way to the top, maybe 30–35 feet up. No problem really, just awkward positioning and initially a bit scary. The barely muffled alternator filled the barn with reverberated sound, miasmic exhaust, and a level of carbon monoxide that I'm sure was not within accepted OSHA standards.

Reaching the top, I struggled to arrange all my tools, rope, and cable; situated myself somewhat precariously on the ladder, hoisted the drill overhead, pressed the trigger, then balanced there with wood shavings cascading over my head and shoulders. Half-a-hole later the drill stopped rotating . . . silence . . . the alternator had quit. Damn!

Picture me balanced at the peak of the roof, cold bare hands overhead grasping the drill, sweater and vest pulled up exposing my mid-rift to the 15°± icebox air, with wood shavings drifting down my neck and working their way into my jockeys . . . and no juice, not a happy camper. I had no alternative but to descend and find out why my power source had shut down. Mentally I was already cursing the custodial people who had provided me with a near-empty alternator. I should have checked . . . I should have stayed home.

By the time I inched my way back down to the floor, the physical and emotional output, had warmed me. But warmth or cold was suddenly not important as I stood, then rotated at the base of the ladder, subconsciously registering that something was wrong. You know how it is when something is *so* wrong that you don't recognize the obvious? The unplugged end of the extension cord was near the base of the ladder, and all I could think of was, "Why is the plug end of the cord here? I'm sure I left the drill stuck in the beam." A quick look up affirmed the drill and attached cord's position where I had left it thirty feet above. "Wait . . . that means . . . *Where's the alternator?*" The 90 pound, not-so-portable electric power pack was gone.

I quickly scanned the floor of the barn, but the large dirty-red machine was no where to be seen. The acrid exhaust practically stuck to my clothes, reminding me that whoever had taken it couldn't have gotten far.

I ran to the double sliding barn doors and in my haste to catch the thieves (it would take at least *two* people to run off with that chunk of dead weight) folded back one of my finger nails while jerking the door open. I was really aggravated now. The newly fallen snow immediately outside the doors revealed no sign of entry or egress. I sprinted to the only other entrance; still no sign of entry or exit—no tracks. Are they still in the barn?

Standing, profoundly befuddled at barn center, with shafts of God-light from cracks and knot holes filtering through the exhaust-filled air, and surrounded by silence, the hairs on the back of my neck prickled; anger shaded towards apprehension. What the hell's going on here?

I quickly searched every square wooden foot of weathered floor and found nothing, not a clue as to where that heavy piece of machinery had gone. The cold silence had become overwhelming, frightening. I looked at my watch; 9:35 AM . . . LUNCH TIME— I'm outta here!

A tracker would have noticed that my boot marks in the snow indicated someone leaving the barn in a hurry.

Dénouement

I returned an hour later with a posse (ostensibly to help lift something, but what I really wanted was some company in that barn). No one could figure out what happen to the "possessed" alternator, as speculation about aliens, deceased former inhabitants, and telekinetic bovines entertained the group for hours. No one seemed overly concerned, puzzled certainly, but quite willing to accept the fact that someone (something), had "eaten" a large machine literally out from under me. The buildings and grounds department reluctantly provided me with another machine (they had to rent one) convinced that I was in cahoots with an alternator rip-off ring.

I finished the job, the weather warmed up into the 20's, and the post-construction training session was well received. In fact, I was enjoying myself so much working with that particular hearing impaired group, I missed my flight back to Boston and had to stay another night.

Two weeks later I received a phone call that solved the mystery of the missing alternator. So, this is *the rest of the story* . . .

Most alternators are not dainty, smooth running machines, and this particular one was an old hyper-vibrating, snorting example of that ill-combusting genre. While I was occupied on the ladder, the vibration of the alternator caused it to "walk" toward a small rectangular hatch opening in the floor that was formerly used to dump "muck" (straw and offal from the animal pens). The ill-balanced, out-of-sync machine, resembling a gigantic wind-up toy, waddled and vibrated about twenty feet toward the hatch, pitched through the opening, pulling its own cord during the ten foot free-fall, then practically covered itself in old muck. The cord rebounded back to the foot of the ladder and silence reigned.

Someone found the alternator during a scheduled clean-up day at the barn about a week after I had left. I was relieved to find out what had happened, but admittedly a bit disappointed that the answer was so mundane. So it wasn't a UFO, an example of telekinesis, or any type of Steven King scenario, just a simple, vibrating, mechanical dance across the floor, and subsequent plunge to an offal ending.

This vignette is no BS, even though that's where the alternator ended up. I hope that's where they left it.

CONCEPTUAL REALITY

Over the years I have used the *PDQ* ploy (**Bottomless Bag Again !?**; pg. 151) to impel participants toward unknown experiences, potentially uncomfortable experiences, and divers other simplistic things-to-do that flirt with the F word (fail).

After having asked the participants to perform some basically simple tasks (snapping fingers, popping their cheek with a levered index finger, whistling, etc.) I announce that the next task is entirely conceptual, only they will know if success is achieved. "Yeah!", they say. "Right on!", I reply.

I'm not going to just verbalize this, try it yourself—take a chance, no one's looking. Touch the tips of your two index fingers together so that they meet about 18" in front of your face. A successful juxtaposing of index digits results in a small link-sausage appearing between your finger tips. See the photo above if you're having trouble "seeing". Is that too much, or what?

INSIDE-OUT UNDERWEAR (BB)

The racy **bold** rubric above caught your eye, eh? Well, scotch those tawdry thoughts, the following is simply a comfort factoid I chanced upon and want to share, because who else is going to regale you with underwear info. To wit:

Wearing your underwear inside out is considerably more comfortable than right side out.

You say, so what? I say, you spend a lot of time in underwear, why not be as comfortable as possible. There's lots of other sartorial fashion gimmicks that are designed for discomfort (neck ties, dress shirts, pointy toed shoes, high heels), so try this simple unseen switch. Tomorrow morning (You don't have to commit right now) put your briefs/panties on inside out. Why? Manufacturers always put seams and labels on the inside of clothing I guess to remind you when your eyes are half open/closed in the early AM, that you are putting your undies on right-side or wrong-side. Also they want to make sure you look good in the mirror wearing their clothes, and with your seams sticking out, you obviously don't look like the half-naked guy in GQ magazine.

But, realistically, who's going to see you in your underwear? OK . . . right, so wear them seams-in for those special occasions, but most of the time try the seams-out positioning: *you will thank me for this.* If you happen to get into an auto accident and the EMT's are whispering about your underwear being on

WRONG, well . . . there has to be a certain amount of risk in adventuring.

As a result of the inchoate rationale above, did you interpret why seams-out is more comfortable than seams-in? It'll be obvious when you switch, but even minimal seams stitched onto comparatively tight clothing will press uncomfortably against your bod. I'll bet you are so used to this excrescence of the tailor's trade that you don't even recognize the discomfort.

This evening when you disrobe, check out the epidermal area around your waist where the label and seams ride. Notice any reddish intaglio marks? Hah! See what I mean?

It doesn't make quite as much difference with your underwear shirt—comfort I mean—and with a shirt, seams-out is more obvious to passerbys, or if you're being *close*. So, if you can't handle everyone mentioning that your shirt is on WRONG or BACKWARD, stick with the briefs crossover only.

Guys, if you wear military style boxer shorts you are largely exempt from seam discomfort, although I can't believe you would wear anything so loose, the wedgie-from-your-friends potential is just too great.

Seams-out could lead to a fad, so restrict this underwear tip to your best friends and family. If some manufacturer got hold of this sartorial insight, every teenager on M/TV would be flaunting their "seams-out" underwear, and I'd have to switch back, just to be different.

TEAM CREAM (BB)

I don't know if I should be telling you about this game because of its purely aggressive roots and because it smacks of gratuitous violence, but I played it with a group of 8th graders and have to admit enjoying the mayhem. Be aware that this game is not for everyone and can be injurious to just about every bone in your body if played to the max with adrenaline-pumped 8th graders. I escaped with a couple bruises and a strained shoulder.

The predecessor for *Team Cream* is a well known and generally disliked playground activity that's truly unorganized and barely authorized. The object of play (?) is for one of the participants (there are no teams per se and a minimum of self enforced rules) to maintain possession of the object of play (usually a nerf football, but it could be anything from a rolled up towel to an empty plastic pop bottle) by attempting to run around within the nebulous boundaries until the object of play is forcefully removed from their grasp. Whoever is "lucky" enough to grab the object then attempts to run around willy-nilly until someone (usually more than one) abruptly stops their progress and guides them unceremoniously to the ground.

I think kids like this game because of the me-against-the-world feeling which alternates with the let's-get-'em team emotion. I'm also pretty sure young boys like the rough and tumble action

(females seldom submit to this type of playground mayhem) because adults don't. But youngsters have been pursuing this playground game for generations (didn't you?), so if you want to offer a rule or two that injects some goal orientation and feelings of camaraderie, here's the rules for *Team Cream*.

Outline a rectangular area on beach sand or grass to measure about 50 × 100 feet. DO NOT PLAY THIS GAME ON CONCRETE OR HOT TOP, in fact you're probably better off not playing this game at all, but . . .

- A Nerf football, as mentioned above, makes a good object of play (OOP) but any *soft* object will do.

- Break up into teams of two or three or four.

- The object of the game is to run the OOP up and down the field as many times as possible before the other team takes the object away and begins their own scoring attempt.

- A point is scored each time a team makes a full field run, one end to the other, so if an OOP is retrieved mid-field it must be run to either end before a scoring run can begin.

- There are no time outs, so play continues until . . .

- If a team scores a point, they continue running up and down the field until stopped by the other team.

- After a player is guided to the turf, that player is not required to give up the OOP and can try to give it to a team member. Tickling is allowed, gouging is not.

If the game continues for more than 2–3 minutes, conditioning and pace begin to tell. Most potentially aerobic games intersperse time slots of very intense physical activity with down-times for sucking wind (usually referred to as planning time by out-of-breath wind suckers). A recent study showed that a pro football player spends approximately four minutes of aerobic activity during a sixty minute game, intense activity alternating with restful strategy breaks. There are no "breathing breaks" associated with playing *Team Cream*. As such, half the players can usually be found lying on their backs wondering why the air is so thin on their particular part of the field. I consider myself in better than fair condition, but five minutes of flat out *Team Cream* sent me to the sidelines looking for a higher concentration of oxygen.

For the sake of your body, do not allow blocking of any kind and certainly no blind-side, knee-high tackles. If you want to slow someone down, grab them around the waist and attempt to sit down.

Don't take winning this game seriously and you will have a much safer and enjoyable time. It's a fun game to play with the neighborhood kids on a fall afternoon. I don't think I'd want to "play" with a group of people my own size, particularly if they were serious about winning.

PANTY HOSE PEREGRINATIONS

The following facts, off-the-hose comments, and sheer speculation are based on two things:

- Spending 10 bucks and a stamp for a cardboard box filled with more reject panty hose legs than you can imagine using, then . . . See the L'Eggs address below. Send a check for $10 and the request for "waste hose" on your non-profit letterhead.

- Writing to Glenn Bannerman to find out what to do with all those cut-off white tubes.

When your box arrives, role play Scrooge McDuck by pulling out gobs and clots of panty hose, festooning them over your head and shoulders, luxuriating in the awareness that you have more of something than you know what to do with.

If it's winter time, pull a panty hose onto each leg to act as a crotchless set of long Johns. Pull one onto each arm also. (If your name is Tom, call them Long Toms, or whatever.) Dye them. Pull one over your head then down over your face. Try to look in the mirror—"Your money, or your life!" With a panty hose on each arm, connect with another person who is also so encumbered, or with an entire group. Use them as people connectors for the initiative game, *Knots* or *Tangle*. Ball up a half

dozen of the hose and stuff them into a separate hose that has one end tied off. Spin it around and throw it like a Comet Ball. Design a May Pole arrangement. If you are playing a team game and don't have pinnies to differentiate players, ask one team to don a flowing white headband from the box. Interested in more?

Glen has a video for sale in which he passes along lots of neat-o things to do with your overflowing box of white stuff. (. . . like trying to push all the removed hose back into the box.) Send Glen a card and ask for details. Tell 'em Karl sent you. Here's the two addresses that you need to know:

Glen Bannerman
Creative Nylon Hoseplay
Box 399
Montreat NC 28757

Sara Lee Hosiery
L'Eggs Products
1901 North Erby St
Florence SC 29501

DRAGON (DRAGGIN') CHAINS

About 15 years ago, during a ropes course construction job, I was dragging a 100' length of 3/8" diameter cable across a football field. I distinctly remember how difficult and satisfying the "pull" was, also wondering at the time if there was a fitness application.

Three years ago I salvaged a couple old 20 foot sections of discarded cable, swaged an eye in the ends, and, using a carabiner, hooked those two lengths into a rock climbing belt. I drove down to my favorite running venue (the beach) and dragged the cables through soft sand, marveling at the increased workout potential and the number of incredulous stares I was receiving.

Since then I've discovered that sections of chain function better than cable, and that attaching a length of 1/4" bungee cord twixt runner and chain allows a smoother run.

This is the real thing folks. If you run on the beach, grass, or a dirt trail you will be impressed at the C-V and BPM increase over your normal run. After a couple runs I predict that you too will experience what I call the "sled dog mentality",

an overwhelming need to get out there and PULL.

Dragon Chains are not only useful toward increasing the intensity of your workout, but it's fun. As you run along in the soft sand take an occasional look

Photo by Dave Klim

over your shoulder. Imagine that the writhing half-buried chain is a sand worm from DUNE—better run faster!

I've been using a 1/2" diameter, 12 link chain at the beach for about 18 months now, and I'm convinced that my current level of fitness is, to a large extent, the result of dragging that chain through the sand. I also use the *Dragon Chain* set-up for running over trails and grass fields, but the pull in soft sand is obviously greater.

The set up includes a 2" webbing waist belt that attaches with velcro, a non-locking carabiner that clips into a climbing loop on the belt, and a ten foot length of 1/4" bungee cord that connects the belt to the length of chain. The bungee cord dampens occasional chain tension and protects the runner in case the chain gets struck on a branch, rock, etc.

There is a gentle pull at the waist (measured at 4 1/2 lbs. for the 12 link chain—I used a fish scale for the measurement) but not so much that it changes your stride noticeably, at least not at the beginning of the run. I run about three miles through soft sand dragging the chain, and toward the end of the run I notice that my breathing and BPM (POLAR heart monitor) are consistently at a higher rate than they would be otherwise. My stride is definitely shorter toward the end of the run.

If you want to increase the workout, simply add more links of chain, with additional lengths of bungee as it seems necessary. Attempting to stride 100 meter repeats down the beach or a grass field pulling four lengths of chain

(48 links) is enough to make any football player's legs and lungs cry for mercy.

A friend of mine that uses a *Dragon Chain* regularly as part of his fitness regimen calls it *The Equalizer*, because it allows him to run with people that he would normally leave in the dust. I have noticed recently that it also provides an increased workout for walkers.

If you want to know more about *Dragon Chains* (I don't sell them) give me a call at the Vermont Project Adventure office and I'll tell you whatever I can. But I'd recommend that you just read the above, get psyched by the photo, and give it a try. Let me know about any interesting vignettes that you experience associated with dragging a chain; share.

XYZ POTPOURRI

In past publications I have included lists of acronyms, categories and Have you ever . . . items, but all under separate headings. I've decided in this issue of FUNN STUFF to include a few from each category, all together under one heading: *XYZ Potpourri*.

Have You Ever . . . (Bottomless Bag Again !?; pg. 127)

. . . seen a Golden Eagle soaring?

. . . dived for a Pamper Pole/Plank trapeze suspended at over 100 feet?

. . . used up an entire tube of lip gloss (Chap Stick) by yourself?

. . . water skied barefoot?

. . . been to the top of Wyoming's Grand Teton?

. . . been inside the sleeping compartment of an 18 wheeler?

. . . dated someone ten years younger than yourself?

. . . been inside a meat packing plant?

. . . gone 36 years without eating a pork-based hot dog?

. . . made a quilt from scratch?

. . . sealed a zip lock bag on the first try?

. . . had something or someone named after you?

. . . actually put together a Mr. Potato Head by yourself?

. . . performed a back hand-spring?

. . . received a senior citizen discount? Aaargh!

Acronyms (*FUNN STUFF Vol. 1; pg. 93*)

HAZMAT — Hazardous Material

RICE — Rest-Ice-Compression-Elevation

NICE — No Intelligent Conversation Emitted

FORD — Found On the Road Dead or Fixed Or Repaired Daily

T.E.A.M — Teachers of Experiential and Adventure Methodology — Theological Expressions in Art and Ministry — Together Everyone Achieves More — Teams Evolve Around Me

PIG — Professional Interest Group or Pretty Intelligent Girl

BFO — Blinding Flash of the Obvious

BUDWEISER — Because U Deserve What Every Individual Should Enjoy Regularly

SIDS — Sudden Infant Death Syndrome

NASCAR — National Association of Stock Car Auto Racing

GED —General Education Diploma

SSN — Social Security Number

TCBY — This Can't Be Yogurt

AEB — As Evidenced By

TNT — Turner Network Television

NBC — Nuclear, Biological & Chemical

RDA — Recommended Daily Allowance

MRE — Meal Ready to Eat

DILLIGAF — Do I Look Like I Give A Flip

Categories (*Bottomless Bag Again ?!; pg. 143*)

- How do you take off a T-shirt or a pull-over jacket? By pulling from the back and over the head with both hands, crossing your arms and pulling overhead, or removing one arm at a time?

- When you are recording the number of times something has been done and you mark down four vertical parallel lines to measure the number, which direction do you apply the fifth diagonal line?

• When you brush your teeth, in which quadrant of your mouth do you start the brushing process? And, do you hold the toothbrush with bristles up or bristles down when you apply the toothpaste?

• Do you regularly sleep with one pillow or two?

• What kind of mattress do you sleep on? Spring? Fouton? Foam? Water? Polymer? What?

• When you start driving, do you put your seat belt on before or after you actually start to drive?

• Get into groups as to what it is you say when you answer the phone. This can be funny so provide time for sharing responses.

PAMPER POLE AND PLANK— AN HISTORIC PERSPECTIVE

The idea for this well known high ropes course event appeared full blown in the fall of 1973.

I was lying in bed one morning (that hypnopompic time just before awakening) when the whole climb/jump scenario materialized. I've had to struggle to make some construction ideas work, but this one was so purely bizarre, so reasonably unreasonable, I knew right away . . .

I was employed at the time as a "staff associate" for a fledgling non-profit educational company called Project Adventure, and it certainly was, the daily adventure being, "What are we going to do today?" Our headquarters (where we tried to figure what was going to happen each day) was located at the Hamilton-Wenham Regional High School, in Hamilton, MA. The 1973 staff of four, plus secretary, was located entirely within one class room, just off the school library.

The ropes course had been completed (whatever that means) a couple years earlier and was being used with considerable success by the PA and high school staff. During the early 70's, trial and error curriculum manipulation/ creation represented the daily lesson plan, as we tried to fulfill our professional teaching duties and the madates of a substantial government grant. As by-products of such pedagogic permissiveness, many new ropes course elements were created. Some of these events faded quickly, others became favorites and a few became classics— the Pamper Pole was one of those few.

When I arrived at work that morning I mentioned the idea to one of the Hamilton-Wenham physical education teachers (Jennifer Simone nee Swisher). Her eyes got big, her smile got bigger and she laughed—I could hardly wait . . .

A previously installed Two Line Bridge element (overengineered with 1/2" cable), provided the overhead support from which I hung the trapeze. The Two Line Bridge belay cable also served as the Pamper Pole belay cable.

I cut down (selective pruning) a nearby, straight-trunked hardwood tree that seemed to offer a challenging height, and with student help levered the potential pole upright into a previously dug post hole. The top of this original oak trunk, that measured maybe 25' from the ground, had a 12" × 12" platform bolted on. As of this writing, I still have the rotted stump of that first pole visually pin-pointed—it's just in front of the rotted stump of pole #2.

The trapeze (fashioned from an unpeeled section of hickory limb, and hung from two spliced lengths of yellow polypropylene rope) hung about seven feet away.

I felt morally obligated (self-imposed at the time, now more or less standard) to take a dive for the trapeze and miss on purpose, in order to test the belay system; it worked. I'm sorry to say I forget who was belaying me. Whoever it was, thanks, I appreciated the support.

That first jump and the multiple leaps-of-faith that followed during the next ten years or so, were belayed by the old single-bowline-around-the-waist. It's interesting how accustomed and dependent people in the field have become toward using a full body harness or Studebaker Wrap to make that trapeze dive. I occasionally tie on a "single bowline", in anticipation of taking a well calculated miss, just to watch the shocked expressions and hear the unbelieving comments. Of course, the Studebaker wrap pelvic support is considerably more comfortable to wear in case of a wide-eyed, leg-pumping drop, but I miss the black and

white simplicity of earlier ways and days. There were less misses back then.

Double belays (two ropes/two belayers) for the well protected trapeze flyer are now in use at some high thrill/low skill locations. And, believe it or not, triple belays are being over-used by at least one organization, in conjunction with a full body harness; he chortled in his sarcasm.

The high pole at Hamilton-Wenham Regional was used for a couple years before Newburyport High School asked us to build one for them indoors. Since then, this event and it's variations have been reproduced by the hundreds, perhaps thousands, world wide. I suspect the Pamper Pole has caused

more wet palms and pants than any other single ropes course event.

The name *Pamper Pole* came about early-on as the result of a fear-induced loosening of a participant's sphincter muscle; the purse-string-like muscle controlling the bladder. That person happened to be wearing kakhi pants at the time, so the dampening was visible even from the ground. A comment made by that good-humored particpant initiated the eventual name, "I sure could have used a set of Pampers."

Here's a few facts and vignettes surrounding the first 20 years of Pamper Pole jumping.

The highest Pamper Pole I know of is just over 50' high and was installed by a

Project Adventure builder. The lowest pole I've seen is just over 15 feet, and that's too low. Truly, the higher the pole, the safer the jump—increased belayer reaction time, substantially more rope stretch, higher tree-top dampening of the belay cable . . .

The highest Pamper Plank I know of was installed by Adrian Kissler and myself at Alpine Christian Conference Center in Blue Jay, CA. The plank was installed on a Douglas Fir at exactly 100' with the trapeze obviously a few feet higher. (See FUNN STUFF #1; pg. 110, for a dramatic photo of this sky-high trapeze jump.)

The first Pamper Plank was built as an alternative to topping a tree to make a Pamper Pole. It seemed more ecologically sound to build a platform than kill a tree. The first "planks" were simply short platforms, but were extended in length as the geography and tree placement demanded. The longest platform I know of is 13' long and is located at Radford University in Virginia. The plank/platform is easier to dive from because it provides considerably more support than a swaying pole. The challenge remains poignant nonetheless.

The world's only Pamper Plonk (combination plank and pole), was installed on the Hinu Haru challenge course in Japan. See photo, this page.

There have been instances when the initial platform built on a support tree proved to be too short to allow a realistic jump to the trapeze. To alleviate this "too challenging" scenario, *beaver boards* are added to the end of the platform. Two 2" × 6" boards are nailed

and clinched to the end of the platform; parallel to one another, about three inches apart, and extending the necessary measurement beyond the end of the platform. Viewed from below, the two boards (in a wildly imaginative way) resemble beaver teeth. Viewed from

above by the jumper they provide a further indication that this is a crazy event, the instructors are nuts, and what am I doing here?

Jumps and dives I have personally experienced or have seen attempted.

- 180° and 360° spinning jumps to the trapeze, and blindfolded

- Facing away from the trapeze and jumping backward

- Running starts on "Planks"

- Jumping in the dark with head lamps

- Diving to music (Theme from the movie *2001* and Elton John's *Rocket Man*)

- Diving with a Santa Claus suit on; also dressed as Batman

- A successful one arm grab *with no belay help*

- Diving and grabbing a vertical trapeze (one end attached)

- Grabbing a trapeze supported by two bungee cords

- Two people diving simultaneously (separate belays—didn't make it)

QUARTERLY QUOTES

QUARTERLY QUOTES

I don't write a "quarterly" anymore, but *Quarterly Quotes* is easy to say easy to remember, and hard to forget, so the rubric remains. I still write down quotes gleaned from my eclectic reading habit, and enjoy sharing the thought or imagined smile. There are a few multi-line quotes to follow, but I still like the pithy one-liners best; hope you like 'em too.

"Part of the loot went for gambling, part for horses, and part for women. The rest I spent foolishly."

George Raft, on how he spent $10 million

"Practice makes perfect, so be careful what you practice."

Anonymous

"War is one of the constants of history and has not diminished with civilization or democracy. In the last 3,421 years of recorded history only 268 have seen no war."

W.A. Durant

"When you have got an elephant by the hind legs and he is trying to run away, it is best to let him run."

"I care not much for a man's religion whose dog or cat are not the better for it."

Abraham Lincoln

"There is nothing so annoying as to have two people go right on talking when you're interrupting."

Mark Twain

"Nothing in fine print is ever good news."

Andy Rooney

"It's easy to identify people who can't count to ten or read. They're the people in front of you in the supermarket cash-only express lane, writing a check."

Julie Henderson and me

"Human beings are the only creatures on earth that allow their children to come back home."

Bill Cosby

"What do you mean we don't communicate? Just yesterday I faxed you a reply to the recorded message that you left on my answering machine."

The Wall Street Journal

"The newspaper lies, the radio lies, the TV lies, the streets howl with truth."

Henry Miller

PLAY — "Let it be an environment that is accepting and forgiving; and let there be real pressures, and let it make definite and clear-cut demands, and let the demands be flexible; and let there be no formal punishment or long lasting ostracism; and let there be hope of friendship and hope of praise; and let there be abundant physical contact and physical exertion; and let the environment offer a sense of skills and a variety of behaviors that lead to greater pleasure . . . and greater security; and let the rewards be immediate and intrinsic to the activity itself."

George Dennison

"The fight then is never with age; it is with boredom, with routine, with the danger of not living at all. Then life will stop, growth will cease, learning will come to an end. You begin to kill time or live it without thought or purpose. Everything that is hapiness, all that is excitement, whatever you know of joy and delight, will evaporate. Life will be reduced to a slow progression of days and weeks and months. Time will become an enemy instead of a ally."

"Play is where life lives. Where the game *is* the game. At its borders we slip into heresy. Become serious. Lose our sense of humor. Fail to see the incongruities of everything we hold to be important. Right and wrong become problematical. Money, power, position becomes the ends. The game becomes winning. And we lose the good life and the things that play provides."

George Sheehan

"It's hard to be a sour grape when you're with a bunch of cherries."

KER

"A couple's first quarrel is Cupid's laxative."

"Ahh. Little alligators of ecstasy, that's what zippers are."

"The word that allows *yes*, the word that makes *no* possible.
The word that puts free in freedom and takes the obligation out of love.
The word that throws the window open after the final door is closed.
The word upon which all adventure, exhileration, all meaning, all honor depends.
The word no mirror can turn around.
In the beginning was the word and the word was—CHOICE."

Tom Robbins

"I'm messed up in Mexico, livin' on refried dreams."

Country/Western Song

"Visitors welcome, members expected."

Sign in front of a Georgia Baptist Church

". . . but the best thing about the adventure workshop is the sound of people having fun—cheering and laughing and joshing one another, people having fun. Fun is the best thing about adventure."

Anonymous work shop participant

"The great man is he who does not lose his child's-heart.

Mencius 372–289 BC

"If you never budge, don't expect a push."

Malcolm Forbes

"Where would you like to spend eternity? Smoking or non-smoking?

Church advertisement

"I was never good at hide and seek because I'd always make enough noise so my friends would be sure to find me. I don't have anyone to play those games with me anymore, but now and then I make enough noise just in case someone is still looking and hasn't found me yet."

Brian Andreas

"We are complaining about the ants at the picnic while the bears are eating our children."

Blaise Pascal

"A guy in a relationship is like an ant standing on top of a truck tire. The ant is aware that something large is there, but he cannot even dimly comprehend what it is. And if the truck starts moving and the tire starts to roll, the ant will sense that something important is happening, but right up until he rolls around to the bottom and is squashed, the only thought in his tiny brain will be, **Huh**?

Dave Barry

"If you talk to God, you are praying; if God talks to you, you have schizophrenia."

Thomas Szasz

"Such an extraterrestrial would be unlikely to see the world as we do. It may be blind, and it may learn about the world through a highly developed sense of smell, or temperature, or pressure. There might be no way to communicate with such a creature, no common ground at all. As one man put it, how would you explain Wordsworth's poem about daffodils to a blind watersnake."

Michael Crichton

"Inch by inch, life's a cinch; yard by yard, life is hard."

Passed on by Jim Wall

". . . monkeys do not talk, because they know if they utter even a single word some man will come and put them to work."

Carl Sagan

"One of the real beauties of bungee jumping is that it allows an insiders look at suicide."

Andrew Rice

"Talent is God given, be humble; fame is man-given, be thankful; conceit is self-given, be careful."

Anonymous

"You don't run 26 miles at five minutes per mile on good looks and a secret recipe."

Frank Shorter

"If you're not making mistakes then you're not doing anything. I'm positive that a doer makes mistakes."

John Wooden

"Competition provides the spice that makes the game fun—but too much spice can make you sick."

KER et al

"Time flies like an arrow. Fruit flies like a banana."

Groucho Marx

FREQUENTLY ASKED QUESTIONS ABOUT THE BOOKS

Silver Bullets, Cowstails & Cobras II,
The Bottomless Bag, Again!?,
QuickSilver, and Funn Stuff
— by Karl Rohnke —

Which of these titles should I pursue if I'm just getting started in adventure education?

Silver Bullets offers over 160 games, initiative problems, trust activities and stunts that have been teacher tested. There is occasional reference made to curriculum use and rationale, but this book was written for practitioners in the field (teachers, recreation specialists, mental health practitioners, Boy & Girl Scout leaders, etc.) who need a collection of adventure education activities that work.

Which book is best for curriculum development?

Cowstails and Cobras II also has many games and initiatives included, but there is a stronger emphasis on techniques and actual curriculum application. Selected adventure programs, from elementary to college level, have been highlighted. These model program chapters have been authored by teachers that are actually implementing the featured program on a day to day basis. However, all the books including games, initiatives, etc. are generic enough to allow program planning by adapting the activities to meet the curriculum needs.

What's *The Bottomless Bag Again!?*

This 400+ page book represents compiled material from Karl's (now out of print) quarterly publication, **Bag of Tricks**. Included are a potpourri of games, initiative problems, ropes course building and implementation information, and whatever else has seemed significant, amusing, or somehow related to adventure education. This book has more information than you can utilize in a semester, unless you're drinking an awful lot of coffee.

How much overlap of activities is there among these books?

There is some overlap between *Silver Bullets* and *The Bottomless Bag Again!?* —I'd guess maybe 30% of rewritten and updated material. There is no duplication between *Silver Bullets* and *Cowstails and Cobras II* that I can remember; the two books are quite different. There is no activity duplication included in *The Bottomless Bag Again!?*, *QuickSilver* and *Funn Stuff*.

Which book came first?

The original *Cowstails & Cobras* (black cover), was published in 1977. *Silver Bullets* — 1984. *Cowstails & Cobras II* — 1991. *The Bottomless Bag Again!?* — 1993. *QuickSilver* — 1995. *Funn Stuff, Vol. 1 & 2* — 1995 & 96.

What other adventure curriculum books have you written?

Cranking Out Adventure — A revised (1992) edition of how to lead a long distance group bicycle trip. This book was published originally in 1976, and I'm pleased that the revision did not involve changing much of the original text; just adding some new technical data and suggesting the use of helmets.

Challenge By Choice — How to build a low challenge ropes course, including a two hour how-to video that complements the book.

Forget Me Knots — How to tie the knots and knot systems specific to ropes course use. Also includes information about rope specs and challenge course applications.

Slightly Skewed Vignettes — *Confessions of an Incorrigible Kid* – Via eighteen autobiographical vignettes, the reader has an opportunity to get a glimpse of the person behind the pen (word processor).

QuickSilver — A sequel to *Silver Bullets*, co-authored with Steve Butler. In addition to more new adventure games, initiatives, etc., includes an extensive section on adventure leadership.

Funn Stuff — A bi-yearly continuation in book form of the quarterly subscription, *Bag of Tricks*. Essentially all the new and good stuff that Karl dreams up and gleans from the field of adventure/experiential education.

All the books are available from *Kendall/Hunt Publishing Co.* Call the following toll free number for prices and ordering information:

1-800-228-0810.

BACK COVER PHOTO

Authoring a book with Kendall/Hunt Publishing Company is a joy for a number of reasons, but the one I appreciate the most is their recognition that, concerning Rohnke books, whimsy and zany are important concepts. Thus the whimsical/zany photo of the author on the back cover, which obviously serves no purpose (certainly not identification) except to allow a smile and wonder.

The photo on the back cover of Volume One was taken by a participant in a workshop I was leading in North Pole, Alaska (a town not far from Fairbanks). Earlier in the workshop (June 1995) I innocently asked, during a break, how could a person urinate outdoors at –40° (Centigrade and Farenheit come together at that temperature). They all laughed but nobody offered an answer, and not really caring,

because I plan to never be outside at –40°, I dropped the subject.

During a get-together after the workshop, the participants in the clinic gave me a very nice T-shirt (see photo) AND a beaver, *fur-lined jock strap,* (also see photo; look carefully). Having regaled me with such Alaskan finery (and humor) they of course wanted to record the moment. The next thing I know I'm being provided with a fur-lined parka, a high powered rifle, snow shoes, a beaver hat and an appropriate sled-type Alaskan dog. The camera shutters sounded like a field of crickets. Is that whimsical or what? Flat out funny too.

The photo on the back cover of Volume #2 (this book) will be fully explained in Volume #3. Kinda gives you something to look forward to, or back toward . . .

P.S. Yes. The photo on page 37 *is* oriented upside down. I just like the way it looked.